BOXER
FUN IS OUR BUSINESS

www.booksbyboxer.com

Bee Three Books

Bee Three Publishing is an imprint of Books By Boxer
Published by
Books By Boxer, Leeds, LS13 4BS, UK
Books by Boxer (EU), Dublin, D02 P593, IRELAND
Boxer Gifts LLC, 955 Sawtooth Oak Cir, VA 22802, USA

cs@boxer.gifts

MADE IN MALTA
ISBN: 9781917954075

FSC
www.fsc.org
MIX
Paper | Supporting responsible forestry
FSC® C022612

This book is produced from responsibly sourced paper to ensure forest management

WELCOME TO DEATH ROW RECIPES

THE RECIPE BOOK THAT TELLS YOU HOW TO MAKE FOOD TO DIE FOR.
WITH RECIPES FOR THE LAST MEALS OF OVER 40 CRIMINALS, AND OVER 70 RECIPES, LEARN MORE ABOUT THE LIFE AND CRIMES OF AMERICA'S DEADLIEST PRISONERS, ALL WHILE MAKING THEIR LAST MEAL ON EARTH.

THE DEATH PENALTY

THE DEATH PENALTY (OR CAPITAL PUNISHMENT) IS LEGAL IN 27 STATES IN AMERICA, WITH THE REMAINING 23 AND WASHINGTON D.C, HAVING ABOLISHED IT.

IT IS USUALLY RESERVED FOR THE MOST SERIOUS OF CRIMES, SUCH AS AGGRAVATED MURDER OR FELONY MURDER (A MURDER THAT HAS ARISEN FROM THE COMMISSION OF ANOTHER FELONY, SUCH AS KIDNAPPING OR ROBBERY), THOUGH IN SOME CASES, THE DEATH PENALTY HAS BEEN GIVEN FOR NON-DEADLY CRIMES.

THE LAST MEAL

ACROSS THE WORLD, INCLUDING THE UNITED STATES, IT IS A CUSTOMARY TRADITION FOR PRISONERS WHO ARE CONDEMNED TO DIE TO RECEIVE A 'LAST MEAL', NOW MORE OFTEN REFERRED TO BY THE EUPHEMISM 'SPECIAL MEAL'. ALTHOUGH OFTEN CONSIDERED THEIR 'LAST' MEAL, MOST STATES GIVE THE SPECIAL MEAL A DAY OR TWO BEFORE THE EXECUTION – UNUSUALLY, LEADING SOME PRISONERS TO RECEIVE TWO 'LAST' MEALS, WHEN THEIR FIRST EXECUTION IS DELAYED.

IT'S ALSO A COMMON BELIEF THAT PRISONERS WILL RECEIVE ANYTHING THEY ASK FOR WITHOUT LIMIT, WHICH ISN'T THE CASE. SOME STATES HAVE MONETARY VALUE LIMITS, SUCH AS FLORIDA, WHERE THE MEAL MUST BE ABLE TO BE PURCHASED LOCALLY AND FOR A VALUE OF UNDER $40. IN OKLAHOMA, THIS VALUE IS LOWER, AT $25. IF PARTICULAR ITEMS AREN'T ABLE TO BE PROVIDED, THEY'RE OFTEN REPLACED WITH 'SIMILAR' SUBSTITUTES.

IN THIS BOOK, YOU'LL SEE A WIDE RANGE OF LAST MEAL REQUESTS, FROM THE MUNDANE TO THE EXTRAVAGANT TO THE DOWNRIGHT STRANGE. AND, YOU'LL LEARN THE REASON WHY SINCE 2011, TEXAS NO LONGER PROVIDES LAST MEALS TO PRISONERS, INSTEAD GIVING THEM THE PRISON MENU OF THE DAY...

IT'S TIME TO TAKE A TRIP TO DEATH ROW...

BIOGRAPHY-JOHN WAYNE GACY

Last words

"KISS MY ASS"

AKA:	THE KILLER CLOWN
BORN:	03/17/1942
DIED:	05/10/1994 (AGED 52)
CONVICTIONS:	MURDER (33 COUNTS)
PENALTY:	DEATH

ONE OF THE MOST NOTORIOUS SERIAL KILLERS IN AMERICAN HISTORY, JOHN WAYNE GACY BECAME INFAMOUS FOR MURDERING AT LEAST 33 YOUNG MEN AND BOYS IN THE 1970S. HE IS OFTEN KNOWN AS THE "KILLER CLOWN", AS HE PERFORMED AT CHARITY EVENTS AS 'POGO THE CLOWN' THROUGHOUT THE TIME HE WAS KILLING, AND ONCE TOLD A POLICE OFFICER, "YOU KNOW... CLOWNS CAN GET AWAY WITH MURDER."

EARLY LIFE:

- HAD A TROUBLED CHILDHOOD WITH AN ABUSIVE FATHER AND HEALTH PROBLEMS.
- TRIED TO LIVE A CONVENTIONAL LIFE: MARRIED, HAD CHILDREN, AND WAS INVOLVED IN COMMUNITY WORK. WHEN HE AND HIS FIRST WIFE DIVORCED, HE NEVER SAW HER OR HIS CHILDREN AGAIN.
- RAN A SUCCESSFUL CONTRACTING BUSINESS (WHERE HE MET AND HIRED MANY OF HIS VICTIMS), AND BECAME ACTIVE IN LOCAL DEMOCRATIC PARTY POLITICS.

CRIMES (1972-1978):

- GACY LURED HIS VICTIMS—MOSTLY TEENAGE BOYS AND YOUNG MEN—BY OFFERING THEM WORK, POSING AS A POLICE OFFICER, OR INVITING THEM TO HIS HOME.
- HE WOULD SEXUALLY ASSAULT, TORTURE, AND STRANGLE HIS VICTIMS.
- MOST OF THE BODIES WERE BURIED IN THE CRAWL SPACE UNDER HIS HOUSE; WHEN HE RAN OUT OF SPACE, HE BEGAN DISCARDING THEM IN A NEARBY RIVER.

CAPTURE AND TRIAL:

- GACY WAS ARRESTED IN DECEMBER 1978 AFTER A TEENAGE BOY, ROBERT PIEST, WENT MISSING.
- DURING THE INVESTIGATION, POLICE DISCOVERED HUMAN REMAINS ON HIS PROPERTY.
- HE CONFESSED TO KILLING OVER 30 PEOPLE.

CONVICTED OF 33 MURDERS IN 1980

SPENT 14 YEARS ON DEATH ROW

EXECUTED BY LETHAL INJECTION ON MAY 10, 1994, IN ILLINOIS.

LAST MEAL-JOHN WAYNE GACY

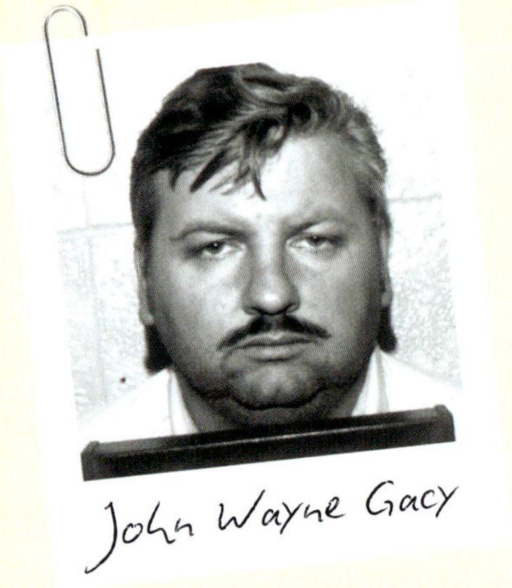

AKA: THE KILLER CLOWN
CRIME: SERIAL MURDER
STATE: ILLINOIS
YEAR: 1994
PUNISHMENT: LETHAL INJECTION

REQUESTED LAST MEAL:

A DOZEN DEEP-FRIED SHRIMP, A BUCKET OF KENTUCKY FRIED CHICKEN, FRENCH FRIES, A POUND OF STRAWBERRIES, AND A BOTTLE OF DIET COKE.

DEEP-FRIED SHRIMP

INGREDIENTS:

- 12 LARGE SHRIMP (PEELED, DEVEINED, TAILS ON OR OFF PER PREFERENCE)
- 125G|1 CUP ALL-PURPOSE FLOUR
- 60G|1/2 CUP CORNSTARCH
- 1 TEASPOON BAKING POWDER
- 1/2 TEASPOON SALT
- 1/2 TEASPOON WHITE PEPPER
- 1/2 TEASPOON GARLIC POWDER
- 1 LARGE EGG, BEATEN
- 120ML|1/2 CUP COLD ICE WATER
- VEGETABLE OIL (FOR DEEP-FRYING)

METHOD

DEEP-FRIED SHRIMP

1. PREPARE THE DRY MIX
   - IN A MEDIUM MIXING BOWL, WHISK TOGETHER THE FLOUR, CORNSTARCH, BAKING POWDER, SALT, WHITE PEPPER, AND GARLIC POWDER.

2. MAKE THE BATTER
   - IN ANOTHER BOWL, WHISK THE BEATEN EGG WITH ICE WATER UNTIL COMBINED.
   - ADD THE LIQUID MIXTURE INTO THE DRY MIX, AND STIR GENTLY.
   - TIP: THE BATTER SHOULD BE SLIGHTLY LUMPY AND THICK ENOUGH TO COAT THE SHRIMP. AVOID OVER-MIXING.

3. HEAT THE OIL
   - IN A DEEP POT OR FRYER, HEAT ENOUGH VEGETABLE OIL TO FULLY SUBMERGE THE SHRIMP.
   - HEAT THE OIL TO 175°C|350°F. USE A THERMOMETER IF POSSIBLE.

4. COAT THE SHRIMP
   - PAT SHRIMP DRY WITH PAPER TOWELS TO HELP THE BATTER STICK.
   - DIP EACH SHRIMP INTO THE BATTER, LETTING EXCESS DRIP OFF SLIGHTLY.

5. FRY THE SHRIMP
   - CAREFULLY LOWER THE BATTERED SHRIMP INTO THE HOT OIL, A FEW AT A TIME TO AVOID OVERCROWDING.
   - FRY FOR 2-3 MINUTES, OR UNTIL GOLDEN BROWN AND CRISPY.

6. DRAIN AND SERVE
   - REMOVE SHRIMP WITH A SLOTTED SPOON AND DRAIN ON A WIRE RACK OR PAPER TOWELS.
   - SPRINKLE WITH A PINCH OF SALT WHILE HOT, IF DESIRED.

7. SERVE IMMEDIATELY
   - SERVE WITH YOUR FAVORITE DIP.

BIOGRAPHY-GERALD EUGENE STANO

Last words:

"I AM INNOCENT. I AM FRIGHTENED. I WAS THREATENED, AND I WAS HELD MONTH AFTER MONTH WITHOUT ANY REAL LEGAL REPRESENTATION. I CONFESSED TO CRIMES I DID NOT COMMIT."

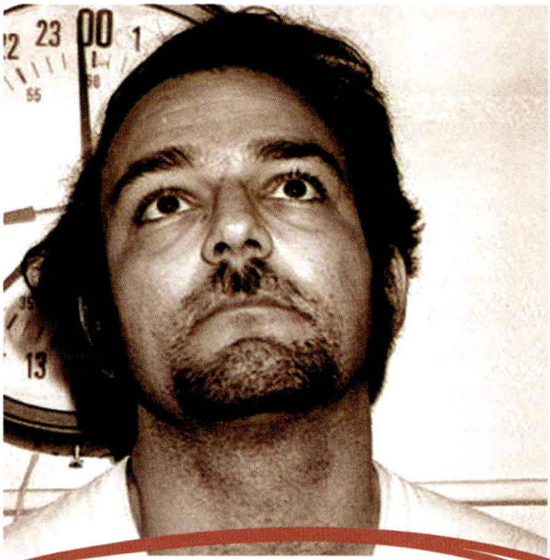

Gerald Eugene Stano

BORN:	09/12/1951
DIED:	03/23/1998 (AGED 46)
CONVICTIONS:	FIRST-DEGREE MURDER (X9)
PENALTY:	DEATH PLUS 8 LIFE SENTENCES

GERALD EUGENE STANO WAS AN AMERICAN SERIAL KILLER WHO CONFESSED TO MURDERING 41 WOMEN ACROSS MULTIPLE STATES, THOUGH HE WAS OFFICIALLY CONVICTED OF 22 MURDERS. HIS CRIMES OCCURRED PRIMARILY DURING THE 1970S. STANO'S CASE IS NOTABLE FOR ITS BRUTALITY, HIS LONG LIST OF CONFESSIONS, AND CONTROVERSY OVER WHETHER ALL HIS CONFESSIONS WERE GENUINE.

EARLY LIFE:

- BORN IN NEW YORK, IN 1951 AS PAUL ZEININGER.
- ABANDONED AT 6 MONTHS OLD (WAS DESCRIBED AS 'UNADOPTABLE', AS HE WAS SO SEVERELY NEGLECTED HE WAS OPERATING AT AN 'ANIMALISTIC LEVEL', EVEN EATING HIS FECES TO SURVIVE), AND THEN ADOPTED BY EUGENE AND NORMA STANO.
- DESCRIBED AS HAVING BEHAVIORAL ISSUES FROM A YOUNG AGE, INCLUDING CRUELTY TO ANIMALS.

CRIMES:

- THE MURDERS PRIMARILY INVOLVED YOUNG WOMEN, OFTEN RUNAWAYS, OR IN VULNERABLE SITUATIONS.
- HIS MODUS OPERANDI TYPICALLY INCLUDED ABDUCTION, FOLLOWED BY STABBING, STRANGULATION, OR BEATING.
- HE WAS ARRESTED IN 1980 AFTER A WOMAN ESCAPED AN ATTACK AND IDENTIFIED HIM.

CAPTURE AND TRIAL:

- WHILE IN CUSTODY, STANO CONFESSED TO 41 MURDERS.
- SOME LAW ENFORCEMENT AGENCIES QUESTIONED WHETHER HE ACTUALLY COMMITTED ALL THE MURDERS HE CONFESSED TO OR WAS SEEKING ATTENTION.
- HE WAS DEFINITIVELY LINKED TO SEVERAL MURDERS THROUGH CORROBORATING EVIDENCE.

CONVICTED OF MULTIPLE MURDERS

SPENT 18 YEARS ON DEATH ROW

EXECUTED IN THE ELECTRIC CHAIR ON MARCH 23, 1998, IN FLORIDA.

LAST MEAL–GERALD EUGENE STANO

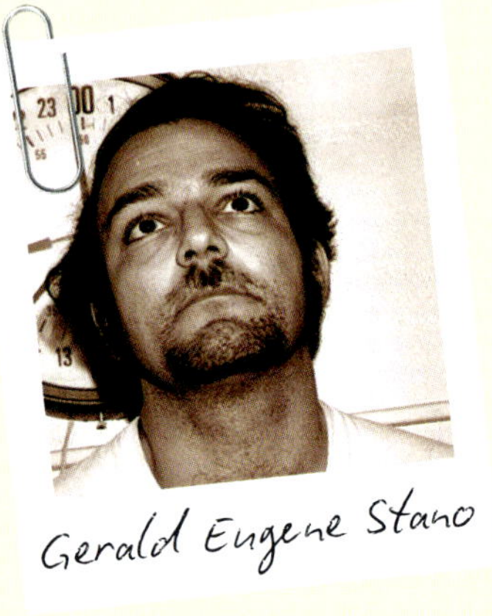

Gerald Eugene Stano

CRIME: SERIAL MURDER
STATE: FLORIDA
YEAR: 1998
PUNISHMENT: ELECTROCUTION

REQUESTED LAST MEAL:

DELMONICO STEAK, A BAKED POTATO WITH SOUR CREAM AND BACON BITS, TOSSED SALAD WITH ROQUEFORT DRESSING, BUTTERED LIMA BEANS, A HALF GALLON OF MINT CHOCOLATE-CHIP ICE CREAM, AND A 2-LITRE BOTTLE OF PEPSI.

DELMONICO STEAK

INGREDIENTS:

- 3 (2.5CM|1-INCH THICK) BONE IN RIBEYE DELMONICO STEAKS, ABOUT 450G|16 OZ
- 3 TEASPOONS KOSHER SALT
- 3 TEASPOONS ANCHO CHILE POWDER
- 1½ TEASPOONS BLACK PEPPER
- 3/4 TEASPOON GARLIC POWDER

LAST MEAL

DELMONICO STEAK

1. SPICE RUB THE STEAKS
    - 1-4 HOURS IN ADVANCE, MIX THE RUB INGREDIENTS IN A BOWL. SPRINKLE OVER THE STEAKS, PLACE STEAK ON A PLATE AND REST IN REFRIGERATOR.

2. SET THE GRILL
    - SET YOUR GRILL FOR DIRECT HIGH HEAT, 230°C|450°F OR HIGHER.

3. GRILL THE STEAKS
    - PLACE THE STEAKS ON THE GRILL OVER DIRECT HIGH HEAT. GRILL FOR 3 MINUTES UNTIL THEY HAVE DARK BROWN GRILLED MARKS ON THE BOTTOM.
    - FLIP AND ROTATE THE STEAKS, GRILL FOR ANOTHER 3 MINUTES. FLIP AND ROTATE AGAIN, GRILL FOR ANOTHER 3 MINUTES.
    - IN THE THICKEST POINT, THEY SHOULD MEASURE 50°C|125°F AND BE MEDIUM-RARE. COOK FOR ANOTHER 1-3 MINUTES IF YOU WANT THEM MORE WELL-DONE.

4. REST THE STEAKS AND SERVE
    - REST FOR 10 MINUTES, THEN SERVE AND ENJOY.

LAST MEAL–BURTON ABBOTT

CRIME:	MURDER AND RAPE
STATE:	CALIFORNIA
YEAR:	1957
PUNISHMENT:	GAS CHAMBER

REQUESTED LAST MEAL:

FRENCH FRIED BUTTERFLY JUMBO PRAWNS WITH COCKTAIL SAUCE, ONE ORDER OF RAVIOLI, TOSSED GREEN SALAD (MAINLY COMPRISED OF ROMAINE LETTUCE) WITH VINEGAR-AND-OIL DRESSING, CHOCOLATE CAKE AND A PACK OF SALEM CIGARETTES.

RAVIOLI

INGREDIENTS:

- 300G|10.6 OZ '00' FLOUR
- 2 EGGS (PLUS 2 EGG YOLKS)
- 1 TABLESPOON OLIVE OIL
- 2 GARLIC CLOVES, CRUSHED
- 200G|7 OZ GARLIC CLOVES, CRUSHED
- 200G|7 OZ BABY SPINACH
- 1/2 LEMON, ZESTED
- NUTMEG, FOR GRATING
- 250G|8.8 OZ RICOTTA
- 50G|1.8 OZ BUTTER
- HANDFUL OF SAGE LEAVES
- GRATED PARMESAN
- SQUEEZE OF LEMON JUICE

RAVIOLI

METHOD

1. MAKE THE PASTA DOUGH
   - MIX FLOUR, EGGS, AND YOLKS IN A BOWL UNTIL A DOUGH FORMS. KNEAD ON A SURFACE FOR 10-15 MINUTES UNTIL SMOOTH. WRAP AND REST FOR 30 MINUTES.

2. MAKE THE SPINACH FILLING
   - SAUTÉ GARLIC IN OIL FOR 30 SECONDS, ADD SPINACH AND A SPLASH OF WATER. COOK UNTIL WILTED AND DRY. ADD LEMON ZEST, NUTMEG, SEASON, AND COOL.

3. ROLL THE PASTA
   - DIVIDE DOUGH INTO 4 PIECES. ROLL EACH THROUGH A PASTA MACHINE FROM WIDEST TO THINNEST. KEEP UNUSED DOUGH COVERED; DUST PASTA AND MACHINE AS NEEDED.

4. MIX THE FILLING
   - STIR RICOTTA INTO COOLED SPINACH. SEASON AND SET ASIDE (OR CHILL).

5. ASSEMBLE THE RAVIOLI
   - CUT PASTA SHEET IN HALF. PLACE FILLING IN TEASPOONS, 5CM|2" APART. BRUSH WITH WATER, LAY SECOND SHEET ON TOP, PRESS TO SEAL AROUND FILLING.

6. CUT THE RAVIOLI
   - BOIL SALTED WATER. ADD RAVIOLI AND COOK 2-3 MINUTES. DRAIN AND COOK IN BATCHES IF NEEDED.

8. MAKE THE BUTTER SAUCE & SERVE
   - BROWN BUTTER WITH SAGE UNTIL CRISP. REMOVE FROM HEAT, TOSS WITH RAVIOLI, PARMESAN, LEMON JUICE, AND PEPPER. SERVE WITH EXTRA PARMESAN.

BIOGRAPHY-CARYL CHESSMAN

CARYL CHESSMAN WAS AN AMERICAN CONVICTED CRIMINAL AND AUTHOR WHO BECAME INTERNATIONALLY FAMOUS AS A DEATH ROW INMATE. HIS CASE ATTRACTED GLOBAL ATTENTION BECAUSE HE WAS SENTENCED TO DEATH UNDER CALIFORNIA'S CONTROVERSIAL "LITTLE LINDBERGH LAW"-WITHOUT KILLING ANYONE-RAISING MAJOR QUESTIONS ABOUT THE USE OF THE DEATH PENALTY IN NON-HOMICIDE CRIMES.

BORN:	05/27/1921
DIED:	05/02/1960 (AGED 38)
CONVICTIONS:	KIDNAPPING, ROBBERY, RAPE
PENALTY:	DEATH

EARLY LIFE:

- BORN IN ST. JOSEPH, MICHIGAN, IN 1921; GREW UP IN CALIFORNIA.
- HAD A TROUBLED YOUTH MARKED BY PETTY CRIME, CAR THEFT, AND GANG INVOLVEMENT.
- IN AND OUT OF JUVENILE DETENTION AND PRISON THROUGHOUT HIS EARLY LIFE.
- BECAME A SKILLED CRIMINAL, OFTEN USING ALIASES AND COMMITTING ROBBERIES AND KIDNAPPINGS.

CRIMES AND ARREST:

- IN 1948, CHESSMAN WAS ARRESTED AND ACCUSED OF BEING THE SO-CALLED "RED LIGHT BANDIT", A MAN WHO USED A RED LIGHT TO IMPERSONATE POLICE AND ABDUCT WOMEN FROM THEIR CARS IN LOS ANGELES.
- HE WAS CHARGED WITH KIDNAPPING, ROBBERY, AND SEXUAL ASSAULT.
- THOUGH NO MURDERS WERE COMMITTED, HE WAS CONVICTED UNDER THE LITTLE LINDBERGH LAW, WHICH ALLOWED FOR A DEATH SENTENCE IF A VICTIM WAS KIDNAPPED AND BODILY HARM OCCURRED.

TRIAL AND CONTROVERSY:

- HIS CASE DREW WIDESPREAD INTERNATIONAL MEDIA ATTENTION, AND BECAME A SYMBOL FOR OPPONENTS OF THE DEATH PENALTY.
- HE WROTE SEVERAL BOOKS (NOTABLY CELL 2455, DEATH ROW) WHILE ON DEATH ROW.

EXECUTION:

- HIS EXECUTION WENT FORWARD DESPITE GLOBAL APPEALS FOR CLEMENCY, INCLUDING FROM ALBERT SCHWEITZER, ELEANOR ROOSEVELT, AND EVEN THE POPE.
- A LAST-MINUTE STAY OF EXECUTION WAS REPORTEDLY GRANTED, BUT IT CAME SECONDS TOO LATE.

SENTENCED TO DEATH IN 1948.

SPENT 12 YEARS ON DEATH ROW.

EXECUTED IN A GAS CHAMBER ON MAY 2, 1960, IN CALIFORNIA.

LAST MEAL–CARYL CHESSMAN

CRIME: KIDNAPPING, RAPE AND ROBBERY
STATE: CALIFORNIA
YEAR: 1960
PUNISHMENT: GAS CHAMBER

REQUESTED LAST MEAL:

A HAM & CHEESE SANDWICH AND A BOTTLE OF COCA-COLA.

INGREDIENTS:

HAM AND CHEESE SANDWICH

- FOUR 1CM|1/2"-THICK SLICES CRUSTY BREAD OR SANDWICH BREAD
- 2 TABLESPOONS MAYONNAISE OR SOFTENED UNSALTED BUTTER, DIVIDED
- 8 THIN SLICES CHEDDAR CHEESE
- 170ML | 6 OZ THINLY SLICED HAM, DIVIDED
- 8 TO 12 PICKLE CHIPS, OPTIONAL

BOTTLE OF COCA-COLA

- BOTTLE OF COCA-COLA

HAM AND CHEESE SANDWICH

1. PREP THE BREAD
   - SPREAD 1 TEASPOON OF MAYONNAISE OR BUTTER ON ONE SIDE OF EACH BREAD SLICE (4 TOTAL).

2. ADD THE FILLING
   - PLACE 2 SLICES OF CHEESE ON EACH SLICE OF BREAD, ON THE BUTTERED/ MAYO SIDE.
   - ADD HAM AND PICKLE CHIPS (IF USING), DIVIDING EVENLY.
   - TOP WITH 2 MORE SLICES OF CHEESE ON EACH.

3. CLOSE THE SANDWICHES
   - SPREAD 1 TEASPOON MAYO ON ONE SIDE OF THE REMAINING BREAD SLICES, THEN SPREAD MUSTARD ON TOP OF THAT.
   - PLACE ON SANDWICHES, MUSTARD SIDE DOWN.
   - PRESS FIRMLY WITH A SPATULA TO SEAL.

BOTTLE OF COCA-COLA

1. PURCHASE BOTTLE OF COCA-COLA
   - PURCHASE BOTTLE OF COCA-COLA.

2. SERVE
   - SERVE AND ENJOY.

LAST MEAL-DEMETRIUS TERRENCE FRAZIER

CRIME: MURDER AND RAPE
STATE: ALABAMA
YEAR: 2025
PUNISHMENT: NITROGEN HYPOXIA

REQUESTED LAST MEAL:

A BEEFY FIVE-LAYER BURRITO, A CHICKEN CHALUPA SUPREME, BEEF CRUNCHY TACOS, CHIPS AND DIP, AND A MOUNTAIN DEW, ALL FROM TACO BELL.

BEEFY FIVE-LAYER BURRITO

INGREDIENTS:

- 450G|1 LB GROUND BEEF
- 1 TABLESPOON ALL-PURPOSE FLOUR
- 2 TABLESPOON TOMATO PASTE
- 1 PACKET TACO SEASONING
- 8 LARGE FLOUR TORTILLAS
- 260G|1 CUP NACHO CHEESE
- 1 CAN REFRIED BEANS
- 240G|1 CUP SOUR CREAM
- 120G|1 CUP SHREDDED CHEDDAR

METHOD

BEEFY FIVE- LAYER BURRITO

1. COOK THE BEEF

- ADD GROUND BEEF TO A NON-STICK PAN OVER MEDIUM-HIGH HEAT.
- COOK UNTIL BROWNED, BREAKING IT INTO SMALL PIECES. NO OIL NEEDED.

2. SEASON THE BEEF

- ONCE COOKED, ADD FLOUR, TOMATO PASTE, TACO SPICES, AND 60ML|¼ CUP WATER.
- STIR AND SIMMER UNTIL THE SAUCE THICKENS. REMOVE FROM HEAT.

3. WARM THE FILLINGS

- HEAT THE NACHO CHEESE AND REFRIED BEANS UNTIL WARM.

4. PREP THE TORTILLAS

- WRAP TORTILLAS IN DAMP PAPER TOWELS AND MICROWAVE FOR 30 SECONDS.
- SPREAD WARM NACHO CHEESE ON HALF THE TORTILLAS.

5. BUILD THE BURRITOS

- TOP WITH THE REMAINING TORTILLAS TO FORM CHEESY TORTILLA SANDWICHES.
- ADD REFRIED BEANS, SEASONED BEEF, SOUR CREAM, AND SHREDDED CHEDDAR ON TOP.

6. WRAP AND SERVE

- FOLD IN THE SIDES, THEN THE BOTTOM, AND ROLL TIGHTLY INTO BURRITOS.
- SLICE IN HALF AND SERVE WARM.

Andrew Reid Lackey

CRIME: MURDER
STATE: ALABAMA
YEAR: 2013
PUNISHMENT: LETHAL INJECTION

REQUESTED LAST MEAL:

TURKEY BOLOGNA, FRENCH FRIES, AND GRILLED CHEESE.

HOME MADE FRENCH FRIES

INGREDIENTS:

- 1KG|2 LB FLOURY POTATOES (MARIS PIPER/KING EDWARD/ RUSSET/IDAHO)
- 2 TABLESPOONS WHITE VINEGAR
- 1 TABLESPOON COOKING SALT
- 1 LITRE|QUART CANOLA / VEG OIL

LAST MEAL

HOME MADE FRENCH FRIES

METHOD

1. PREP THE POTATOES
   - PEEL THE POTATOES AND CUT INTO 6MM|¼ INCH FRENCH FRIES.
   - KEEP CUT FRIES IN A BOWL OF WATER WHILE YOU WORK TO PREVENT BROWNING.

2. RINSE THE FRIES
   - TRANSFER FRIES TO A COLANDER AND RINSE UNDER COLD WATER FOR 15–20 SECONDS.

3. SIMMER THE FRIES
   - PLACE FRIES IN A LARGE POT WITH 2 LITRES (OR QUARTS) OF COLD WATER, A SPLASH OF VINEGAR, AND SALT.
   - BRING TO A BOIL, THEN REDUCE TO A GENTLE SIMMER.
   - COOK FOR 10 MINUTES, THEN REMOVE GENTLY AND PLACE IN A COLANDER.

4. DRY THE FRIES
   - SPREAD FRIES ON TEA TOWEL-LINED TRAYS.
   - LET THEM STEAM-DRY FOR 5 MINUTES.

5. HEAT THE OIL
   - POUR 3CM|1.2 INCHES OF OIL INTO A DEEP POT.
   - ENSURE THERE'S AT LEAST 7CM|3 INCHES OF SPACE FROM OIL TO RIM FOR SAFETY.
   - HEAT TO 205°C|400°F.

6. FIRST FRY (QUICK BLANCH)
   - ADD FRIES TO HOT OIL IN THIRDS, 10 SECONDS APART.
   - FRY FOR 50 SECONDS, AND TRANSFER TO PAPER TOWEL-LINED TRAY.
   - LET FRIES COOL FOR 30 MINUTES.

7. SECOND FRY (CRISPING)
   - REHEAT OIL TO 205°C|400°F.
   - FRY FRIES IN TWO BATCHES, 4 MINUTES EACH, STIRRING TWICE.

BIOGRAPHY-LAWRENCE RUSSELL BREWER

LAWRENCE RUSSELL BREWER (1967-2011) WAS AN AMERICAN WHITE SUPREMACIST AND CONVICTED MURDERER. HE BECAME NATIONALLY KNOWN FOR HIS ROLE IN THE 1998 RACIALLY MOTIVATED MURDER OF JAMES BYRD JR., ONE OF THE MOST HORRIFIC HATE CRIMES IN MODERN U.S. HISTORY. THE CRIME SHOCKED THE NATION AND LED TO SIGNIFICANT CHANGES IN HATE CRIME LEGISLATION.

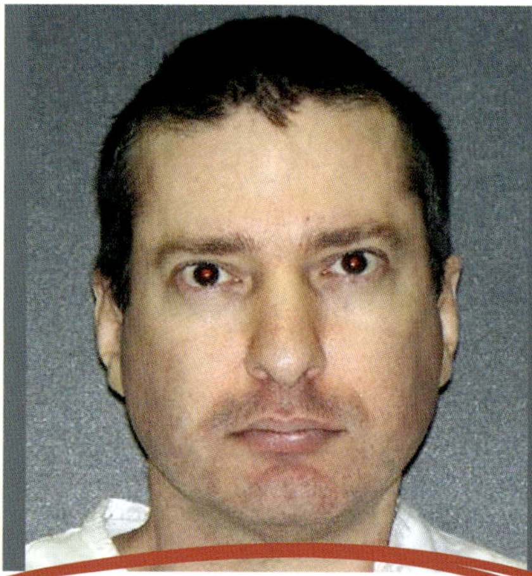

Lawrence Russell Brewer

BORN:	03/13/1967
DIED:	09/21/2011 (AGED 44)
CONVICTIONS:	MURDER
PENALTY:	DEATH

EARLY LIFE:

- BORN IN FOLLANSBEE, WEST VIRGINIA, IN 1967.
- RAISED IN TEXAS, HIS EARLY LIFE WAS MARKED BY DRUG USE, CRIMINAL BEHAVIOR, AND WHITE SUPREMACIST AFFILIATIONS.
- SPENT TIME IN AND OUT OF PRISON, WHERE HE REPORTEDLY JOINED A WHITE SUPREMACIST GANG FOR PROTECTION.

THE CRIME:

- ON JUNE 7, 1998, IN JASPER, TEXAS, BREWER AND TWO OTHER WHITE MEN—JOHN WILLIAM KING AND SHAWN BERRY—OFFERED A RIDE TO JAMES BYRD JR., A 49-YEAR-OLD BLACK MAN WHO WAS WALKING HOME.
- INSTEAD OF TAKING HIM HOME, THEY BEAT HIM SEVERELY, CHAINED HIM BY THE ANKLES TO THE BACK OF A PICKUP TRUCK, AND DRAGGED HIM FOR NEARLY THREE MILES ALONG A RURAL ROAD.
- BYRD DIED AFTER HIS BODY STRUCK A CULVERT, AND HIS REMAINS WERE SCATTERED ALONG THE ROAD.

ARREST AND TRIAL:

- ALL THREE MEN WERE ARRESTED SHORTLY AFTER.
- BREWER WAS TRIED IN 1999. HE SHOWED NO REMORSE.
- HE WAS CONVICTED OF CAPITAL MURDER AND SENTENCED TO DEATH.
- WHEN ASKED BY A JOURNALIST IF HE HAD REGRETS, HE SAID, "NO, I HAVE NO REGRETS. NO, I'D DO IT ALL OVER AGAIN, TO TELL YOU THE TRUTH."

EXECUTION:

- BREWER WAS EXECUTED BY LETHAL INJECTION IN 2011.
- HE MADE HEADLINES AGAIN BY ORDERING AN EXTRAVAGANT LAST MEAL (WHICH HE DIDN'T EAT), PROMPTING TEXAS TO END THE PRACTICE OF ALLOWING INMATES TO CHOOSE THEIR FINAL MEALS.

SENTENCED TO DEATH IN 1999.

SPENT 10 YEARS ON DEATH ROW.

EXECUTED BY LETHAL INJECTION ON SEPTEMBER 21, 2011, IN TEXAS.

CRIME: MURDER
STATE: TEXAS
YEAR: 2011
PUNISHMENT: LETHAL INJECTION

LAST 'FINAL MEAL' REQUEST IN TEXAS

REQUESTED LAST MEAL:

TWO CHICKEN FRIED STEAKS SMOTHERED IN GRAVY WITH SLICED ONIONS, A TRIPLE MEAT BACON CHEESEBURGER WITH FIXINGS ON THE SIDE, A CHEESE OMELET WITH GROUND BEEF, TOMATOES, ONIONS, BELL PEPPERS, AND JALAPEÑOS, A LARGE BOWL OF FRIED OKRA WITH KETCHUP, ONE POUND OF BARBECUE WINGS WITH HALF A LOAF OF WHITE BREAD, THREE FAJITAS WITH FIXINGS, A MEAT LOVERS PIZZA, THREE ROOT BEERS, ONE PINT OF BLUE BELL VANILLA ICE CREAM, AND A SLAB OF PEANUT BUTTER FUDGE WITH CRUSHED PEANUTS. IT WAS GRANTED, BUT HE REFUSED TO EAT ANY BECAUSE HE 'WASN'T HUNGRY', BRINGING AN END TO SPECIAL MEAL REQUESTS IN TEXAS.

FRIED OKRA WITH KETCHUP

INGREDIENTS:

- 450G|1 LB FRESH OKRA PODS
- 2 EGGS
- 1½ TEASPOON KOSHER SALT
- VEGETABLE OIL, FOR FRYING
- 195G|1¼ CUPS YELLOW CORNMEAL
- 40G|1/4 CUP ALL-PURPOSE FLOUR
- 1/2 TEASPOON BLACK PEPPER
- 1/4 TEASPOON CAYENNE PEPPER

LAST MEAL

FRIED OKRA WITH KETCHUP

1. PREP THE OKRA
   - TRIM STEMS AND THIN TIPS FROM FRESH OKRA.
   - SLICE INTO 1CM|½-INCH PIECES.

2. SOAK IN EGG
   - IN A BOWL, LIGHTLY BEAT 2 EGGS WITH 1/2 TEASPOON SALT.
   - ADD OKRA AND STIR TO COAT.
   - LET SOAK FOR 10 MINUTES.

3. HEAT THE OIL
   - IN A CAST-IRON SKILLET, HEAT 2CM|3/4 INCH OF OIL TO 190°C|375°F.

4. MIX THE BREADING
   - IN A LARGE ZIP-TOP BAG, COMBINE:
   - CORNMEAL; FLOUR; 1 TEASPOON SALT; BLACK PEPPER; AND CAYENNE PEPPER (OPTIONAL).
   - SEAL AND SHAKE TO MIX.

5. COAT THE OKRA
   - REMOVE OKRA FROM EGG MIXTURE WITH A SLOTTED SPOON, LETTING EXCESS DRAIN OFF.
   - ADD TO BAG WITH BREADING.
   - SEAL BAG WITH SOME AIR INSIDE AND SHAKE TO COAT.

6. FRY THE OKRA
   - WORKING IN 2 BATCHES, FRY OKRA IN HOT OIL FOR 2-3 MINUTES, UNTIL GOLDEN BROWN.
   - TRANSFER TO A PAPER TOWEL-LINED PLATE.

7. SEASON AND SERVE
   - SPRINKLE WITH EXTRA SALT IF DESIRED.
   - SERVE HOT WITH KETCHUP ON THE SIDE.

LAST MEAL-CHARLES BROOKS JR

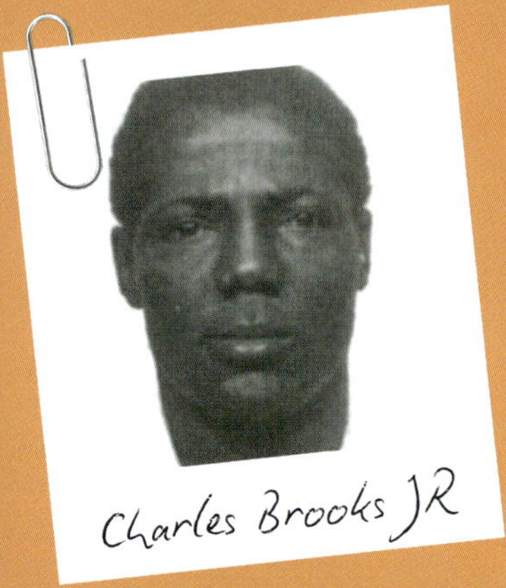

CRIME: MURDER
STATE: TEXAS
YEAR: 1982
PUNISHMENT: LETHAL INJECTION

REQUESTED LAST MEAL:

A T-BONE STEAK, FRENCH FRIES, KETCHUP, WORCESTERSHIRE SAUCE, BISCUITS, PEACH COBBLER, AND ICED TEA. ORIGINALLY HE HAD REQUESTED FRIED SHRIMP AND OYSTERS, BUT THE PRISON CHEF TOLD HIM SHELLFISH WASN'T AN OPTION.

PEACH COBBLER

INGREDIENTS:

- 2 CANS SLICED PEACHES
- 120G|4.25 OZ GOLDEN SUGAR
- 1 TSP GROUND GINGER
- 150G|5.3 OZ PLAIN FLOUR
- 1 TEASPOON BAKING POWDER
- 1/2 TEASPOON GROUND CINNAMON
- 150G|5.3 OZ BUTTER
- 1 SMALL EGG

METHOD

PEACH COBBLER

1. PREP THE PEACHES

- PREHEAT OVEN TO 180°C|350°F
- GREASE A BAKING DISH WITH BUTTER.
- ADD DRAINED PEACH SLICES, SPRINKLE WITH 2 TBSP SUGAR AND A PINCH OF GINGER. SET ASIDE.

2. MAKE THE DOUGH

- IN A FOOD PROCESSOR, COMBINE FLOUR, REMAINING SUGAR, BAKING POWDER, CINNAMON, AND A PINCH OF SALT.
- ADD BUTTER AND PULSE UNTIL MIXTURE LOOKS LIKE BREADCRUMBS.
- ADD EGG AND BLITZ UNTIL A THICK DOUGH FORMS.

3. ASSEMBLE & BAKE

- SPOON DOUGH IN DOLLOPS OVER THE PEACHES, LEAVING SMALL GAPS.
- SPRINKLE WITH CASTER SUGAR.
- BAKE FOR 40 MINUTES UNTIL GOLDEN.
- SERVE WARM AND ENJOY.

Last words

"YES, I DO.
I LOVE YOU.
ASDADU AN LA ILAH ILLA ALLAH,
ASDADU AN LA ILAH ILLA ALLAH,
ASDADU ANNA MUHAMMADAN RASUL ALLAH,
ASDADU ANNA MUHAMMADAN RASUL ALLAH.
I BEAR WITNESS THAT THERE IS NO GOD BUT ALLAH. I BEAR WITNESS THAT MUHAMMAD IS THE MESSENGER OF ALLAH. INNA LI-ALLAH WA-INNA ILAYHI RAJIUN. VERILY UNTO ALLAH DO WE BELONG, VERILY UNTO HIM DO WE RETURN. BE STRONG."

BIOGRAPHY-IGNACIO CUEVAS

IGNACIO CUEVAS (1939-1991) WAS EXECUTED IN TEXAS FOR HIS ROLE IN THE 1974 HUNTSVILLE PRISON SIEGE THAT RESULTED IN THE DEATHS OF TWO HOSTAGES. THE INCIDENT WAS ONE OF THE MOST DRAMATIC AND DEADLY HOSTAGE CRISES IN U.S. PRISON HISTORY.

BORN:	07/31/1931
DIED:	05/23/1991 (AGED 59)
CONVICTIONS:	FIRST-DEGREE MURDER (2 COUNTS)
PENALTY:	DEATH

EARLY LIFE:

BORN IN 1939 IN TEXAS, OF MEXICAN-AMERICAN HERITAGE. GREW UP IN POVERTY AND HAD LIMITED EDUCATION; REPORTEDLY HAD A TROUBLED YOUTH WITH INVOLVEMENT IN PETTY CRIMES. BY THE EARLY 1970S, HE WAS SERVING A LONG SENTENCE FOR MURDER AT THE TEXAS STATE PENITENTIARY IN HUNTSVILLE.

THE CRIME:

- ON JULY 24, 1974, CUEVAS PARTICIPATED IN A HOSTAGE-TAKING AT THE HUNTSVILLE "WALLS UNIT" PRISON, ALONGSIDE FRED GÓMEZ CARRASCO, A DRUG KINGPIN, AND RUDOLFO DOMÍNGUEZ, ANOTHER INMATE.
- THE MEN SMUGGLED FIREARMS INTO THE PRISON AND TOOK OVER THE PRISON LIBRARY, HOLDING OVER 15 HOSTAGES.
- THE SIEGE LASTED 11 DAYS AND ON AUGUST 3, 1974, THE INMATES ATTEMPTED TO ESCAPE USING A CHALKBOARD AND HOSTAGES AS HUMAN SHIELDS INSIDE A MAKESHIFT BULLETPROOF BARRIER.
- A SHOOTOUT WITH LAW ENFORCEMENT ENSUED. CARRASCO AND DOMÍNGUEZ WERE KILLED; CUEVAS SURVIVED.
  TWO HOSTAGES WERE KILLED: JULIA STANDLEY, A PRISON EDUCATOR, AND ELIZABETH BESEDA, A VISITING TEACHER.

ARREST & TRIAL:

- CUEVAS WAS CHARGED WITH CAPITAL MURDER FOR THE DEATHS OF THE HOSTAGES.
- IN 1975, HE WAS CONVICTED AND SENTENCED TO DEATH.
- CUEVAS DENIED FIRING ANY SHOTS DURING THE CONFRONTATION, BUT HE WAS HELD RESPONSIBLE UNDER THE LAW OF PARTIES, ALLOWING CAPITAL PUNISHMENT FOR ACCOMPLICES.

EXECUTION:

- EXECUTED BY LETHAL INJECTION ON MAY 23, 1991, AT THE HUNTSVILLE UNIT IN TEXAS.
- EXPRESSED REMORSE BEFORE HIS DEATH AND ACKNOWLEDGED THE PAIN CAUSED TO THE VICTIMS' FAMILIES.
- HIS EXECUTION CLOSED A CHAPTER ON ONE OF TEXAS'S MOST INFAMOUS PRISON UPRISINGS.

CONVICTED OF 2 MURDERS IN 1975.

SPENT 16 YEARS ON DEATH ROW.

EXECUTED BY LETHAL INJECTION ON MAY 23, 1991, IN TEXAS.

LAST MEAL-IGNACIO CUEVAS

CRIME: PERPETRATOR OF THE 1974 HUNTSVILLE PRISON SIEGE
STATE: TEXAS
YEAR: 1991
PUNISHMENT: LETHAL INJECTION

REQUESTED LAST MEAL:

CHICKEN AND DUMPLINGS, STEAMED RICE, BLACK-EYED PEAS, AND ICED TEA.

CHICKEN AND DUMPLINGS

INGREDIENTS:

- 1 TABLESPOON OLIVE OIL
- 90G|2 LBS BONE-IN SKINLESS CHICKEN BREAST OR THIGHS
- SALT AND PEPPER, TO TASTE
- 5 TABLESPOONS BUTTER
- 1 SMALL YELLOW ONION, DICED
- 125G|1 CUP CARROTS, DICED
- 2 STICKS CELERY, DICED
- 3 GLOVES GARLIC, MINCED
- 1 TEASPOON WORCESTERSHIRE SAUCE
- 1 TEASPOON HOT SAUCE
- 40G|1/3 CUP FLOUR
- 1L|4½ CUPS CHICKEN BROTH
- 1 CHICKEN BOUILLON CUBE
- 360ML|1½ CUPS HALF AND HALF
- 115G|3/4 CUP FROZEN PEAS

SEASONINGS

- 1 TEASPOON ONION POWDER
- 1/2 TEASPOON EACH: DRIED BASIL, PARSLEY, THYME, ROSEMARY, MUSTARD POWDER
- 1/4 TEASPOON GROUND SAGE
- 1/8 TEASPOON PEPPER

DUMPLINGS

- 250G|2 CUPS ALL-PURPOSE FLOUR
- 2 TEASPOONS BAKING POWDER
- 1/2 TEASPOON BAKING SODA
- 1 TEASPOON SALT
- 1/2 TEASPOON GARLIC POWDER
- 2 TEASPOONS SUGAR
- 180ML|3/4 CUP COLD SOUR CREAM
- 60ML|1/4 CUP COLD MILK
- 4 TABLESPOONS BUTTER, MELTED

CHICKEN AND DUMPLINGS

METHOD

1. SEAR THE CHICKEN (OPTIONAL)

- SEASON CHICKEN WITH SALT AND PEPPER.
- HEAT OIL IN A LARGE POT OVER MEDIUM-HIGH.
- SEAR CHICKEN 3 MINUTES PER SIDE UNTIL LIGHTLY BROWNED (CENTER WILL BE RAW). REMOVE, REST 10 MINUTES, THEN DICE. DISCARD BONES.

2. COOK THE VEGETABLES AND SEASONINGS

- MELT BUTTER IN THE SAME POT. SCRAPE UP BROWN BITS.
- ADD ONIONS, CARROTS, AND CELERY; COOK 5 MINUTES UNTIL SOFT.
- STIR IN GARLIC, WORCESTERSHIRE, HOT SAUCE, AND SEASONINGS. COOK 1 MINUTE.

3. MAKE THE SOUP BASE

- ADD FLOUR AND COOK 2 MINUTES, STIRRING.
- GRADUALLY ADD BROTH, SCRAPING THE BOTTOM.
- STIR IN HALF & HALF IN SPLASHES.
- ADD BOUILLON IF USING.
- ADD PEAS AND BRING TO A GENTLE BOIL. SIMMER UNCOVERED.

4. MAKE THE DUMPLINGS

- MIX FLOUR, BAKING POWDER, BAKING SODA, SALT, GARLIC POWDER, AND SUGAR.
- ADD MILK, SOUR CREAM, AND MELTED BUTTER.
- FOLD TO FORM A SOFT DOUGH WITHOUT OVERMIXING.

5. ADD CHICKEN AND COOK DUMPLINGS

- STIR DICED CHICKEN INTO SOUP.
- REDUCE HEAT TO LOW AND DROP DUMPLINGS ONTO SOUP WITH A SPOON.
- SPOON A LITTLE SOUP OVER EACH.
- COVER TIGHTLY, SIMMER GENTLY FOR 15 MINUTES WITHOUT LIFTING LID.

6. CHECK AND SERVE

- TEST DUMPLINGS WITH A TOOTHPICK; IF CLEAN, THEY'RE DONE. SIMMER A FEW MORE MINUTES IF NEEDED.
- GARNISH WITH PARSLEY AND SERVE HOT.

BIOGRAPHY–KARLA FAYE TUCKER

"YES, SIR, I WOULD LIKE TO SAY TO ALL OF YOU—THE THORNTON FAMILY AND JERRY DEAN'S FAMILY—THAT I AM SO SORRY. I HOPE GOD WILL GIVE YOU PEACE WITH THIS. [SHE LOOKED AT HER HUSBAND.] BABY, I LOVE YOU. [SHE LOOKED AT RONALD CARLSON.] RON, GIVE PEGGY A HUG FOR ME. [SHE LOOKED AT ALL PRESENT WEEPING AND SMILING.] EVERYBODY HAS BEEN SO GOOD TO ME. I LOVE ALL OF YOU VERY MUCH. I AM GOING TO BE FACE TO FACE WITH JESUS NOW. WARDEN BAGGETT, THANK ALL OF YOU SO MUCH. YOU HAVE BEEN SO GOOD TO ME. I LOVE ALL OF YOU VERY MUCH. I WILL SEE YOU ALL WHEN YOU GET THERE. I WILL WAIT FOR YOU."

Karla Faye Tucker

Last words

BORN:	11/18/1959
DIED:	02/03/1998 (AGED 38)
CONVICTIONS:	CAPITAL MURDER (2 COUNTS)
PENALTY:	DEATH

KARLA FAYE TUCKER (1959–1998) WAS A TEXAS WOMAN CONVICTED OF A BRUTAL DOUBLE MURDER IN 1983. SHE BECAME INTERNATIONALLY KNOWN NOT ONLY FOR THE VIOLENT NATURE OF HER CRIME BUT FOR HER DRAMATIC RELIGIOUS CONVERSION ON DEATH ROW. TUCKER WAS THE FIRST WOMAN EXECUTED IN TEXAS SINCE THE CIVIL WAR AND THE FIRST IN THE U.S. SINCE 1984, DRAWING WIDESPREAD ATTENTION AND SPARKING INTENSE DEBATE OVER REDEMPTION, FORGIVENESS, AND CAPITAL PUNISHMENT.

EARLY LIFE:

- BORN IN HOUSTON, TEXAS, IN 1959.
- HAD A TROUBLED UPBRINGING: BEGAN USING DRUGS AND ALCOHOL AT A YOUNG AGE.
- REPORTEDLY STARTED PROSTITUTING HERSELF AT 14.
- DROPPED OUT OF SCHOOL AND FELL INTO A LIFE OF ADDICTION AND CRIME.
- BECAME INVOLVED WITH DANNY GARRETT, A MUCH OLDER MAN AND FELLOW DRUG USER, IN THE EARLY 1980S.

THE CRIME:

- ON JUNE 13, 1983, TUCKER AND GARRETT BROKE INTO THE APARTMENT OF JERRY LYNN DEAN IN HOUSTON, INTENDING TO STEAL MOTORCYCLE PARTS.
- DURING THE BREAK-IN, TUCKER USED A PICKAXE TO KILL DEAN AFTER GARRETT HAD STRUCK HIM IN THE HEAD WITH A HAMMER. WHEN A WOMAN, DEBRA THORNTON, WAS ALSO FOUND IN THE ROOM, TUCKER ALSO ATTACKED AND KILLED HER WITH THE SAME PICKAXE.
- TUCKER LATER ADMITTED THAT SHE EXPERIENCED A “THRILL” AND “SEXUAL EXCITEMENT” DURING THE KILLINGS, A DETAIL THAT SHOCKED THE PUBLIC.
- THE CRIME WAS EXCEPTIONALLY BRUTAL AND WIDELY PUBLICIZED.

RELIGIOUS CONVERSION AND PUBLIC SYMPATHY:

- WHILE ON DEATH ROW, TUCKER UNDERWENT A CHRISTIAN RELIGIOUS CONVERSION AND CLAIMED TO BE TRULY REMORSEFUL FOR HER CRIMES.
- SHE BECAME A MODEL INMATE, MINISTERED TO OTHERS, AND GAINED A LARGE FOLLOWING OF SUPPORTERS.
- APPEALS FOR CLEMENCY CAME FROM ACROSS THE GLOBE, INCLUDING FROM POPE JOHN PAUL II.

CONVICTED OF CAPITAL MURDER IN 1984

SPENT 14 YEARS ON DEATH ROW

EXECUTED BY LETHAL INJECTION ON FEBRUARY 3, 1998, IN TEXAS.

CRIME: MURDER
STATE: TEXAS
YEAR: 1998
PUNISHMENT: LETHAL INJECTION

REQUESTED LAST MEAL:

A BANANA, A PEACH, AND A SALAD WITH EITHER RANCH OR ITALIAN DRESSING

A SALAD WITH RANCH DRESSING

INGREDIENTS:

DRESSING

- 80ML|1/3 CUP OLIVE OIL
- 240ML|1 CUP SOUR CREAM
- 80ML|1/3 CUP BUTTERMILK
- 1 TABLESPOON FRESH SQUEEZED LEMON JUICE
- 2 TEASPOONS DRIED CHIVES
- 2 TEASPOONS DRIED PARSLEY
- 3/4 TEASPOON GARLIC POWDER
- 3/4 TEASPOON ONION POWDER
- 1/2 TEASPOON DRIED DILL WEED
- 1/4 TEASPOON FRESHLY CRACKED BLACK PEPPER
- 1/4 TEASPOON SALT, TO TASTE

SALAD

- 600G|8 CUPS ROMAINE LETTUCE, WASHED, DRIED, AND TORN INTO PIECES
- 300G|2 CUPS RAW VEGETABLES, CARROTS, BELL PEPPERS, MUSHROOMS, SLICED RED ONION, ETC.

A SALAD WITH RANCH DRESSING

RANCH DRESSING

1. MIX THE DRESSING
   - ADD ALL INGREDIENTS TO A 1 LITRE|QUART MASON JAR.
   - SHAKE WELL UNTIL FULLY COMBINED.
   - OPTIONALLY, BLEND USING A BLENDER FOR A SMOOTHER TEXTURE.

2. ADJUST SEASONING
   - TASTE AND TWEAK FLAVORS AS NEEDED – ADD MORE HERBS, GARLIC, OR SALT IF DESIRED.

SALAD ASSEMBLY

1. PREP THE BASE
   - IN A LARGE BOWL, TOSS TOGETHER LETTUCE AND RAW VEGETABLES OF CHOICE.

2. DRESS THE SALAD
   - ADD RANCH DRESSING AND TOSS TO COAT EVENLY.
   - OR SERVE DRESSING ON THE SIDE FOR INDIVIDUAL SERVINGS.

3. ADD TOPPINGS (OPTIONAL)
   - FINISH WITH HOMEMADE CROUTONS, NUTS, OR SUNFLOWER SEEDS FOR EXTRA CRUNCH.

LAST MEAL–JAMES EDWARD SMITH

CRIME: SERIAL MURDER
STATE: TEXAS
YEAR: 1990
PUNISHMENT: LETHAL INJECTION

REQUESTED LAST MEAL:

A LUMP OF DIRT, MEANT FOR A VOODOO RITUAL, WHICH WAS DENIED. SETTLED FOR A YOGURT INSTEAD.

INGREDIENTS:

HOME MADE YOGHURT

- 500ML|17.5 OZ 2% MILK
- 1 TBSP PLAIN LIVE NATURAL YOGURT

A LUMP OF DIRT

YOU WILL NEED:

- A HAND TROWEL

LAST MEAL

Last words:

"HARE KRISHNA"

HOME MADE YOGHURT

1. HEAT THE MILK

- ADD MILK TO A SMALL, HEAVY-BASED SAUCEPAN.
- HEAT OVER MEDIUM, STIRRING OCCASIONALLY.
- WARM TO 85°C|185°F – MILK SHOULD BE STEAMING WITH SMALL BUBBLES, BUT NOT BOILING.

2. COOL THE MILK

- REMOVE PAN FROM HEAT AND LET MILK COOL TO 46°C|115°F (TAKES APPROX 25-30 MINUTES).

3. ADD THE YOGURT STARTER

- TRANSFER 3 TABLESPOONS OF THE COOLED MILK TO A SMALL BOWL.
- MIX IN THE YOGURT UNTIL SMOOTH.
- POUR THE MIXTURE BACK INTO THE PAN AND STIR TO COMBINE.

4. INCUBATE THE YOGURT

- POUR THE MILK INTO A 500ML|17 OZ FLASK OR CONTAINER.
- SCREW ON THE LID AND LEAVE UNDISTURBED AT ROOM TEMPERATURE FOR AT LEAST 10 HOURS.
- FOR THICKER, TANGIER YOGURT, LET IT SET FOR UP TO 24 HOURS.

5. TRANSFER AND STORE

- ONCE SET, TRANSFER YOGURT TO A STERILISED GLASS JAR AND SEAL.
- STORE IN THE FRIDGE FOR UP TO 2 WEEKS.

A LUMP OF DIRT

1. DIG UP DIRT

- IN A GARDEN OR GRASSY AREA, DIG UP SOME DIRT.

2. STORE

- STORE IN A BOX OR BUCKET

BIOGRAPHY-WANDA JEAN ALLEN

Last words:

"FATHER FORGIVE THEM. THEY KNOW NOT WHAT THEY DO."

Wanda Jean Allen

BORN:	08/17/1959
DIED:	01/11/2001 (AGED 41)
CONVICTIONS:	FIRST-DEGREE MURDER
PENALTY:	DEATH

EARLY LIFE:

- BORN ON AUGUST 17, 1959, IN OKLAHOMA CITY, OKLAHOMA.
- RAISED IN POVERTY AS ONE OF EIGHT CHILDREN; HER MOTHER WAS LARGELY ABSENT AND STRUGGLED WITH ALCOHOLISM.
- SUFFERED BRAIN DAMAGE FROM MULTIPLE HEAD INJURIES AS A TEENAGER, LEADING TO COGNITIVE IMPAIRMENTS AND A LOW IQ.
- DROPPED OUT OF HIGH SCHOOL AND HAD DIFFICULTY MAINTAINING EMPLOYMENT OR STABLE RELATIONSHIPS.

FIRST CRIME:

- IN 1981, ALLEN SHOT AND KILLED HER ROOMMATE AND GIRLFRIEND, DEDRA PETTUS, DURING AN ARGUMENT.
- CLAIMED THE SHOOTING WAS ACCIDENTAL, BUT FORENSIC EVIDENCE CONTRADICTED HER ACCOUNT.
- PLEADED GUILTY TO MANSLAUGHTER AND SERVED TWO YEARS OF A FOUR-YEAR SENTENCE.

THE CRIME:

- IN 1988, ALLEN WAS IN A VOLATILE RELATIONSHIP WITH GLORIA JEAN LEATHERS, A WOMAN SHE MET WHILE BOTH WERE IN PRISON.
- ON DECEMBER 2, 1988, FOLLOWING A HEATED ARGUMENT AND CONFRONTATION AT A GROCERY STORE, LEATHERS WENT TO A POLICE STATION TO FILE A COMPLAINT.
- ALLEN FOLLOWED AND SHOT LEATHERS IN THE PARKING LOT IN FRONT OF WITNESSES.
- LEATHERS DIED FROM HER INJURIES DAYS LATER.

ARREST AND TRIAL:

- ALLEN WAS ARRESTED AT THE SCENE AND CHARGED WITH FIRST-DEGREE MURDER.
- PROSECUTORS EMPHASIZED HER PRIOR CONVICTION AS AN AGGRAVATING FACTOR.
- HER DEFENSE DID NOT ADEQUATELY PRESENT EVIDENCE OF HER MENTAL IMPAIRMENTS DURING THE TRIAL.

CONVICTED OF 1ST DEGREE MURDER, 1989

SPENT 12 YEARS ON DEATH ROW

EXECUTED BY LETHAL INJECTION ON JANUARY 11, 2001, IN OKLAHOMA

LAST MEAL–WANDA JEAN ALLEN

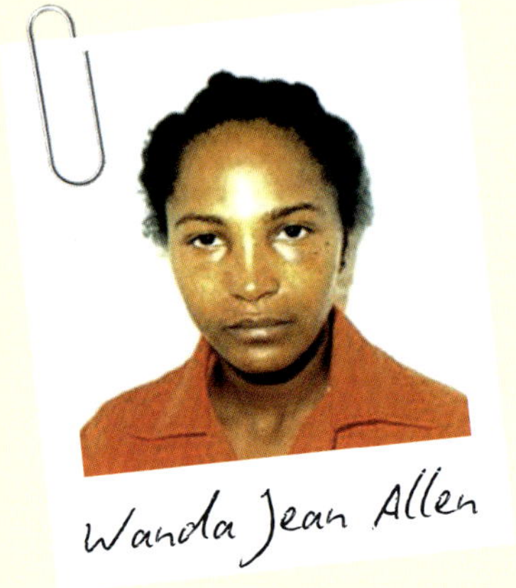

CRIME: MURDER
STATE: OKLAHOMA
YEAR: 2001
PUNISHMENT: LETHAL INJECTION

REQUESTED LAST MEAL:

A BAG OF POTATO CHIPS.

HOMEMADE POTATO CHIPS

INGREDIENTS:

- 1KG|2 LBS RUSSET|MARIS PIPER POTATOES
- 70ML|3 CUPS VEGETABLE OIL
- 1-2 TABLESPOONS SALT

EQUIPMENT:

- MANDOLINE
- DEEP SKILLET
- SLOTTED SPOON
- INSTANT READ THERMOMETER

A BAG OF POTATO CHIPS

1. SLICE THE POTATOES
   - PEEL POTATOES AND SLICE THINLY USING A MANDOLINE AT 2MM|1/16 INCH THICKNESS.
   - TRANSFER SLICES TO A LARGE BOWL.

2. SOAK AND REMOVE STARCH
   - COVER POTATOES WITH COLD WATER AND ADD A HANDFUL OF ICE CUBES.
   - LET SIT FOR 30 MINUTES TO DRAW OUT SURFACE STARCH.

3. DRY THE POTATOES
   - LINE A LARGE CASSEROLE DISH WITH A CLEAN, ABSORBENT TOWEL.
   - DRAIN POTATOES IN A COLANDER AND SHAKE OFF EXCESS WATER.
   - SPREAD A SINGLE LAYER ON THE TOWEL-LINED DISH.
   - PAT DRY WITH ANOTHER CLEAN TOWEL OR PAPER TOWELS.
   - TRANSFER DRIED SLICES TO A BOWL OR PLATE.
   - REPEAT UNTIL ALL SLICES ARE DRY.

4. FRY THE CHIPS
   - HEAT OIL IN A LARGE, DEEP SKILLET TO 175°C|350°F.
   - WORKING IN BATCHES, ADD POTATO SLICES IN A SINGLE LAYER.
   - FRY FOR 3-4 MINUTES, STIRRING CONSISTENTLY WITH A SLOTTED SPOON UNTIL GOLDEN BROWN.

5. DRAIN AND SEASON
   - REMOVE CHIPS FROM OIL AND PLACE ON A PAPER TOWEL-LINED RACK OR PLATE.
   - SPRINKLE WITH SALT WHILE STILL HOT.
   - LET COOL COMPLETELY IN A SINGLE LAYER TO AVOID SOGGINESS.

6. STORE OR SERVE
   - ONCE FULLY COOLED, STORE CHIPS IN AN AIRTIGHT CONTAINER OR SERVE IMMEDIATELY.

BIOGRAPHY-VELMA BARFIELD

Last words:

"I KNOW THAT EVERYBODY HAS GONE THROUGH A LOT OF PAIN, ALL THE FAMILIES CONNECTED, AND I AM SORRY, AND I WANT TO THANK EVERYBODY WHO HAVE BEEN SUPPORTING ME ALL THESE SIX YEARS."

Velma Barfield

BORN: 10/29/1932
DIED: 11/02/1984 (AGED 52)
CONVICTIONS: FIRST-DEGREE MURDER
PENALTY: DEATH

MARGIE VELMA BARFIELD (1932-1984) WAS A SERIAL KILLER AND THE FIRST WOMAN EXECUTED IN THE UNITED STATES AFTER THE REINSTATEMENT OF CAPITAL PUNISHMENT IN 1976. SHE WAS ALSO THE FIRST WOMAN IN THE U.S. TO BE EXECUTED BY LETHAL INJECTION. SHE WANTED TO DONATE HER ORGANS, BUT IT WAS NOT POSSIBLE AS HER HEART WAS UNABLE TO BE RESTARTED. HER CORNEAS AND SOME SKIN TISSUE WERE ABLE TO BE USED.

EARLY LIFE:

- BORN OCTOBER 29, 1932, IN EASTOVER, NORTH CAROLINA.
- SECOND OF NINE CHILDREN, RAISED IN A POOR AND ABUSIVE HOUSEHOLD.
- DROPPED OUT OF SCHOOL IN HER TEENS AND MARRIED AT 17, HAVING TWO CHILDREN.
- FOLLOWING A HYSTERECTOMY, SHE DEVELOPED A SEVERE ADDICTION TO PRESCRIPTION DRUGS.

CRIMINAL ACTIVITY:

- IN 1969, HER FIRST HUSBAND DIED IN A SUSPICIOUS HOUSE FIRE.
- HER SECOND HUSBAND DIED SUDDENLY IN 1971 UNDER MYSTERIOUS CIRCUMSTANCES.
- BETWEEN 1974 AND 1978, SHE POISONED HER MOTHER AND SEVERAL ELDERLY PEOPLE IN HER CARE, OFTEN TO CONCEAL FINANCIAL FRAUD.
- IN 1978, SHE POISONED HER FIANCÉ, ROWLAND “STUART” TAYLOR, WHICH LED TO A CRIMINAL INVESTIGATION.

ARREST & TRIAL:

- ARRESTED ON MAY 13, 1978, AFTER A VICTIM’S AUTOPSY REVEALED ARSENIC POISONING.
- CONFESSED TO MULTIPLE MURDERS BUT WAS TRIED FOR ONLY ONE DEATH.
- CONVICTED OF FIRST-DEGREE MURDER IN DECEMBER 1978 AND SENTENCED TO DEATH.

IMPRISONMENT:

- WHILE ON DEATH ROW, SHE BECAME A DEVOUT BORN-AGAIN CHRISTIAN AND MINISTERED TO FELLOW INMATES.

CONVICTED OF 1ST DEGREE MURDER, 1978.

SPENT 6 YEARS ON DEATH ROW.

EXECUTED BY LETHAL INJECTION ON NOVEMBER 2, 1984, IN NORTH CAROLINA

LAST MEAL–VELMA BARFIELD

CRIME:	MURDER
STATE:	NORTH CAROLINA
YEAR:	1984
PUNISHMENT:	LETHAL INJECTION

REQUESTED LAST MEAL:

DECLINED A SPECIAL MEAL, HAD A BAG OF CHEEZ DOODLES AND A CAN OF COCA COLA INSTEAD.

HOMEMADE CHEESE PUFFS

INGREDIENTS:

CHEESE PUFFS:

- 90G|1/2 CUP TAPIOCA STARCH
- 20G|1/8 CUP FINELY GROUND CORN FLOUR
- 1 TEASPOON SALT
- 1 TEASPOON CANE SUGAR
- 30G|1 OZ GRATED, LOOSELY PACKED SHARP CHEDDAR CHEESE, MELTED WITH 1 TABLESPOON OF WATER
- 30-60ML|1/8-1/4 CUP HOT WATER, PLUS MORE FOR STEAMING
- SAFFLOWER OIL FOR FRYING
- SALT

CHEESE POWDER:

- 60G|2 OZ GRATED CHEDDAR CHEESE
- 1 TEASPOON WATER
- 30-40G|1/4-1/3 CUP TAPIOCA STARCH
- 1/2 TEASPOON SALT
- 1/4 TEASPOON SUGAR

METHOD

CHEESE PUFFS

1. PREPARE THE STEAMER
   - BRING A LARGE POT WITH A STEAMER TRAY TO A BOIL.
   - LINE TRAY WITH LIGHTLY OILED PARCHMENT PAPER.

2. MAKE THE DOUGH
   - IN A FOOD PROCESSOR, COMBINE TAPIOCA STARCH, CORN FLOUR, SALT, SUGAR, AND MELTED CHEESE. PULSE, THEN ADD HOT WATER UNTIL A THICK, STICKY DOUGH FORMS.

3. STEAM THE DOUGH
   - PRESS DOUGH INTO A 7MM|1/4-INCH THICK LAYER ON OILED PARCHMENT.
   - STEAM FOR 45-60 MINUTES UNTIL RUBBERY AND TRANSLUCENT.
   - COOL, THEN FLIP AND DRY SLIGHTLY.

4. SLICE AND DRY
   - CUT INTO STICKS, ROLL GENTLY.
   - DRY IN DEHYDRATOR 6-10 HOURS OR OVEN (LOWEST SETTING, DOOR OPEN) FOR 6-8 HOURS UNTIL CRISP.

CHEESE POWDER

1. PREHEAT THE OVEN
   - PREHEAT TO LOWEST SETTING (75°C-90°C |170°F-200°F).
   - LINE A BAKING SHEET WITH PARCHMENT OR SILICONE MAT.

2. MELT THE CHEESE
   - HEAT CHEESE AND WATER IN A SAUCEPAN OVERMEDIUM-LOW, STIRRING CONSTANTLY UNTIL FULLY MELTED (DO NOT BROWN).

3. MAKE THE CRUMBS
   - TRANSFER TO FOOD PROCESSOR WITH TAPIOCA STARCH AND PULSE UNTIL IT LOOKS LIKE BREADCRUMBS. ADD MORE STARCH IF TOO DOUGHY.

4. BAKE THE CRUMBS
   - SPREAD ON BAKING SHEET. BAKE FOR 45 MINUTES UNTIL DRY THEN COOL FOR 10 MINUTES.

5. BLEND INTO POWDER AND SERVE
   - BLEND WITH SALT AND SUGAR UNTIL FINE. IF MOIST, ADD MORE STARCH AND BLEND AGAIN. COVER CHEESE PUFFS IN POWDER.

LAST MEAL–RODNEY BERGET

CRIME: MURDER
STATE: SOUTH DAKOTA
YEAR: 2018
PUNISHMENT: LETHAL INJECTION

REQUESTED LAST MEAL:

PANCAKES, WAFFLES, MAPLE SYRUP AND BUTTER, BREAKFAST SAUSAGES, SCRAMBLED EGGS, FRENCH FRIES, PESI, AND CHERRY NIBS LICORICE.

WAFFLES

INGREDIENTS:

- 270G|2¼ CUPS ALL-PURPOSE FLOUR
- 50G|1/4 CUP GRANULATED SUGAR
- 1 TABLESPOON BAKING POWDER
- 3/4 TEASPOON SALT
- 480ML|2 CUPS MILK
- 115G|1/2 CUP UNSALTED BUTTER, MELTED
- 2 LARGE EGGS
- 2 TEASPOONS VANILLA EXTRACT

LAST MEAL

CONSIDERED INTELLECTUALLY DISABLED AS HIS IQ SCORE WAS 70

METHOD

WAFFLES

1. PREHEAT THE WAFFLE IRON
   - SET YOUR WAFFLE IRON TO A HIGH OR DARK SETTING FOR EXTRA CRISPY WAFFLES.

2. MIX THE DRY INGREDIENTS
   - IN A LARGE BOWL, WHISK TOGETHER FLOUR, SUGAR, BAKING POWDER, AND SALT.

3. MIX THE WET INGREDIENTS
   - IN A SEPARATE BOWL, WHISK TOGETHER MILK, MELTED BUTTER, EGGS, AND VANILLA.

4. COMBINE THE MIXTURES
   - POUR THE WET MIXTURE INTO THE DRY INGREDIENTS.
   - STIR JUST UNTIL COMBINED – DO NOT OVERMIX.

5. COOK THE WAFFLES
   - GREASE THE HOT WAFFLE IRON WITH BUTTER OR COOKING SPRAY.
   - ADD ABOUT 80ML|1/3 CUP BATTER PER WAFFLE (ADJUST BASED ON YOUR WAFFLE MAKER).
   - COOK UNTIL GOLDEN BROWN.

6. SERVE AND ENJOY
   - PLACE WAFFLES ON A WIRE RACK TO STAY CRISP UNTIL SERVING.
   - SERVE HOT WITH MAPLE SYRUP, BUTTER, OR YOUR FAVORITE TOPPINGS

Last words

"SORRY FOR THE DELAY, I GOT CAUGHT IN TRAFFIC. BUT SERIOUSLY, I WANT TO THANK EVERYBODY THAT WAS THERE FOR ME. I LOVE YOU ALL. UH, SHAKY VOICE. UH, I LOVE YOU TAMMY. I KNOW YOU'RE HERE WITH ME. AND SONNY BOY. I LOVE YOU AND I'LL MEET YOU OUT THERE. I LOVE YOU GIGI."

WHEN INJECTED: "IS IT SUPPOSED TO FEEL LIKE THAT?"

LAST MEAL-ALFRED BOURGEOIS

CRIME: MURDER
STATE: FEDERAL GOVERNMENT
YEAR: 2020
PUNISHMENT: LETHAL INJECTION

REQUESTED LAST MEAL:

SEAFOOD-STUFFED MUSHROOMS, A PLATTER OF FRIED SHRIMP, SHRIMP ALFREDO PASTA, SIX BUTTERED BISCUITS AND CHEESECAKE.

SEAFOOD STUFFED MUSHROOMS

INGREDIENTS:

- 1 PACKAGE CREAM CHEESE, SOFTENED
- 1 GREEN ONION, CHOPPED
- 1 EGG YOLK
- 1 TABLESPOON ITALIAN BREAD CRUMBS
- 1 TABLESPOON LEMON JUICE
- 1 TEASPOON WORCESTERSHIRE SAUCE
- 1 TEASPOON GARLIC POWDER
- 1 PINCH SALT AND GROUND BLACK PEPPER, TO TASTE
- 1 CAN SNOW CRAB, DRAINED
- 1 CAN SMALL SHRIMP, DRAINED
- 12 LARGE WHITE MUSHROOMS, STEMS REMOVED
- 60G|1 CUP ITALIAN BREADCRUMBS

SEAFOOD STUFFED MUSHROOMS

1. PREHEAT THE OVEN

- PREHEAT OVEN TO 200°C|400°F.
- LINE A BAKING SHEET WITH ALUMINUM FOIL.

2. MAKE THE FILLING

- IN A STAND MIXER BOWL, ADD CREAM CHEESE, GREEN ONION, EGG YOLK, 1 TBSP BREAD CRUMBS, LEMON JUICE, WORCESTERSHIRE SAUCE, GARLIC POWDER, SALT, AND BLACK PEPPER.
- BEAT WITH PADDLE ATTACHMENT UNTIL SMOOTH AND WELL BLENDED.
- FOLD IN CRAB AND SHRIMP.

3. STUFF THE MUSHROOMS

- FILL MUSHROOM CAPS WITH THE CREAM CHEESE MIXTURE.
- PRESS REMAINING BREADCRUMBS ON TOP TO COAT.
- PLACE STUFFED MUSHROOMS ON THE BAKING SHEET, STUFFED-SIDES UP.

4. BAKE AND BROIL

- BAKE FOR 12-14 MINUTES UNTIL MUSHROOMS ARE SLIGHTLY SOFTENED.
- TURN ON THE BROILER AND BROIL UNTIL TOPS ARE GOLDEN AND BUBBLY.

LAST MEAL-RUSSELL EARL BUCKLEW

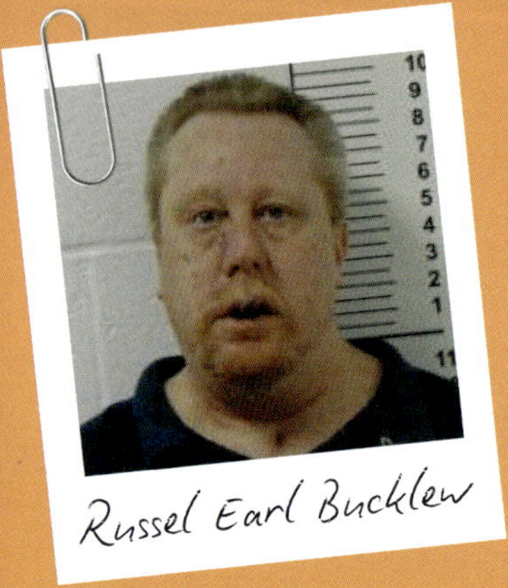

CRIME: MURDER
STATE: MISSOURI
YEAR: 2019
PUNISHMENT: LETHAL INJECTION

REQUESTED LAST MEAL:

A GREEK GYRO, A SMOKED BRISKET SANDWICH, TWO ORDERS OF FRENCH FRIES, COLA, AND A BANANA SPLIT.

GREEK GYROS

INGREDIENTS:

- 1KG|2 LB CHICKEN THIGH FILLETS, BONELESS SKINLESS
- 3 LARGE GARLIC CLOVES, MINCED
- 1 TABLESPOON WHITE WINE VINEGAR
- 3 TABLESPOONS LEMON JUICE
- 1 TABLESPOON EXTRA VIRGIN OLIVE OIL
- 3 TABLESPOONS GREEK YOGURT
- 1½ TABLESPOONS DRIED OREGANO
- 1 TEASPOON SALT
- BLACK PEPPER
- 2 CUCUMBERS, GRATED AND SQUEEZED
- 300ML|1¼ CUPS GREEK YOGURT
- 1 TABLESPOON LEMON JUICE
- 1 TABLESPOON EXTRA VIRGIN OLIVE OIL
- 1 GARLIC CLOVE, MINCED
- 1/4 TEASPOON SALT
- BLACK PEPPER
- 3 TOMATOES, DESEEDED AND DICED
- 3 CUCUMBERS, DICED
- 1/2 RED ONION, FINELY CHOPPED
- 6G|1/4 CUP FRESH PARSLEY LEAVES
- 4 TO 6 GREEK FLATBREADS

GREEK GYROS

METHOD

1. MARINATE THE CHICKEN

- PLACE ALL MARINADE INGREDIENTS IN A ZIPLOCK BAG AND MASSAGE TO COMBINE.
- ADD CHICKEN AND MASSAGE UNTIL FULLY COATED.
- MARINATE FOR AT LEAST 3 HOURS, IDEALLY 12, AND NO LONGER THAN 24 HOURS.

2. MAKE THE TZATZIKI

- CUT CUCUMBER IN HALF LENGTHWISE AND SCRAPE OUT SEEDS WITH A TEASPOON.
- COARSELY GRATE THE CUCUMBER, THEN WRAP IN PAPER TOWELS OR A CLEAN CLOTH AND SQUEEZE OUT EXCESS LIQUID.
- ADD CUCUMBER TO A BOWL WITH THE REMAINING TZATZIKI INGREDIENTS.
- MIX WELL AND SET ASIDE FOR AT LEAST 20 MINUTES TO LET FLAVORS DEVELOP.

3. PREP THE SALAD

- COMBINE ALL SALAD INGREDIENTS IN A BOWL.
- TOSS TO MIX AND SET ASIDE.

4. COOK THE CHICKEN

- BRUSH GRILL WITH OIL AND PREHEAT TO MEDIUM-HIGH. OR HEAT 1 TBSP OIL IN A FRYING PAN OVER MEDIUM-HIGH HEAT.
- REMOVE CHICKEN FROM MARINADE AND COOK FOR 2-3 MINUTES PER SIDE, UNTIL GOLDEN AND COOKED THROUGH.
- TRANSFER TO A PLATE, COVER LOOSELY WITH FOIL, AND REST FOR 5 MINUTES.

5. ASSEMBLE THE GYROS

- IF USING LARGE CHICKEN THIGHS, CUT INTO SMALLER PIECES.
- PLACE WARMED PITA OR FLATBREAD ON A PIECE OF PARCHMENT OR FOIL.
- ADD SALAD DOWN THE CENTER, THEN TOP WITH CHICKEN AND TZATZIKI.
- ROLL UP THE WRAP AND TWIST THE PAPER END TO HOLD IT TOGETHER. CUT IF DESIRED.

LAST MEAL-VICTOR FEGUER

CRIME: MURDER
STATE: FEDERAL GOVERNMENT
YEAR: 1963
PUNISHMENT: HANGING

REQUESTED LAST MEAL:

AN OLIVE WITH THE PIT STILL INSIDE.

SINGLE UNPITTED OLIVE

INGREDIENTS:

- SINGLE UNPITTED OLIVE

METHOD:

1. PLATE UP
   - PLACE OLIVE ON PLATE
2. SERVE
   - SERVE AND ENJOY!

WHEN QUESTIONED ON HIS CHOICE OF LAST MEAL IT'S CLAIMED THAT FEGUER HAD TOLD GUARDS HE HOPED A OLIVE TREE WOULD GROW FROM HIS GRAVE 'AS A SIGN OF PEACE'. SOME REPORTS STATE AFTER HIS EXECUTION GUARDS FOUND THE SINGLE OLIVE PIT IN THE POCKET OF HIS SUIT, WHETHER HE WAS ACTUALLY BURIED WITH IT IS UNKNOWN.

LAST MEAL–ROBERT ANTHONY BUELL

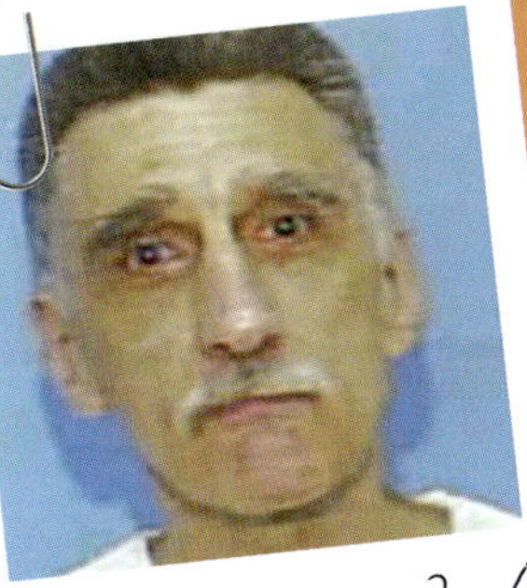

Robert Anthony Buell

CRIME: MURDER
STATE: OHIO
YEAR: 2002
PUNISHMENT: LETHAL INJECTION

REQUESTED LAST MEAL:

A SINGLE, UNPITTED BLACK OLIVE.

LAST MEAL

SINGLE UNPITTED OLIVE

INGREDIENTS:

- SINGLE UNPITTED OLIVE

METHOD:

1. PLATE UP
   - PLACE OLIVE ON PLATE
2. SERVE
   - SERVE AND ENJOY!

Last words

"JERRY AND SHIRLEY, I DIDN'T KILL YOUR DAUGHTER. THE PROSECUTOR KNOWS THAT... AND THEY LEFT THE REAL KILLER OUT THERE ON THE STREETS TO KILL AGAIN AND AGAIN AND AGAIN. SO THAT SOME GOOD MAY COME OF THIS, I ASK THAT YOU CONTINUE TO PURSUE THIS TO THE END. DON'T LET THE PROSECUTOR CONTINUE TO SPIN THIS OUT OF FOCUS AND FORCE THEM TO FIND OUT WHO REALLY KILLED YOUR DAUGHTER. THAT'S ALL I HAVE TO SAY."

LAST MEAL–THOMAS J GRASSO

CRIME: MURDER
STATE: OKLAHOMA
YEAR: 1995
PUNISHMENT: LETHAL INJECTION

REQUESTED LAST MEAL:

TWO DOZEN STEAMED MUSSELS, TWO DOZEN STEAMED CLAMS, A DOUBLE CHEESEBURGER FROM BURGER KING, HALF-DOZEN BARBECUED SPARE RIBS, TWO STRAWBERRY MILKSHAKES, HALF A PUMPKIN PIE WITH WHIPPED CREAM, AND DICED STRAWBERRIES, AND A CAN OF SPAGHETTIOS.

STEAMED MUSSELS

INGREDIENTS:

- 900G|2 LBS MUSSELS, CLEANED
- 1 TABLESPOON BUTTER
- 2 SMALL SHALLOTS, THINLY SLICED
- 2 GARLIC CLOVES, FINELY CHOPPED
- 240ML|1 CUP CHICKEN STOCK
- 120ML|1/2 CUP DRY WHITE WINE
- SPLASH HEAVY CREAM
- 6G|1/4 CUP FRESH PARSLEY, ROUGHLY CHOPPED
- SALT AND PEPPER
- LEMON WEDGES, FOR SERVING
- 1 BAGUETTE, WARMED FOR SERVING

STEAMED MUSSELS

1. COOK SHALLOTS & GARLIC

- MELT BUTTER IN A LARGE POT OVER MEDIUM HEAT.
- ADD SHALLOTS AND GARLIC, COOK UNTIL SOFTENED (ABOUT 5 MINUTES).

2. ADD LIQUIDS & MUSSELS

- POUR IN CHICKEN STOCK AND WHITE WINE.
- ADD MUSSELS AND TOSS.
- COVER WITH LID AND COOK FOR 6–10 MINUTES UNTIL MUSSELS OPEN.
- DISCARD ANY THAT STAY CLOSED.

3. FINISH THE BROTH

- REMOVE FROM HEAT. STIR IN CREAM AND CHOPPED PARSLEY.
- TASTE AND SEASON WITH SALT, PEPPER, OR MORE CREAM IF NEEDED.

4. SERVE

- SPOON INTO BIG BOWLS.
- SERVE WITH LEMON WEDGES AND WARM BREAD TO SOAK UP THE BROTH.

AN HOUR BEFORE HE DIED, HE ISSUED HIS FOURTH AND FINAL STATEMENT:

"I DID NOT GET MY SPAGHETTIOS,
I GOT SPAGHETTI.
I WANT THE PRESS TO KNOW THIS."

BIOGRAPHY-SCOTT CARPENTER

IN FINAL WRITTEN STATEMENT:

"I TELL THE YOUNG AND OLD, DO NOT STRAY ONTO THE WRONG PATH IN LIFE AS I DID. I SPEAK FROM EXPERIENCE WHEN I SAY IT'S A LONG AND BUMPY ROAD, WITH A LOT OF REGRET AND FEW SECOND CHANCES."

BORN:	01/02/1975
DIED:	05/08/1997 (AGED 22)
CONVICTIONS:	FIRST-DEGREE MURDER
PENALTY:	DEATH

SCOTT DAWN CARPENTER (1975-1997) WAS A CONVICTED MURDERER AND THE YOUNGEST PERSON EXECUTED IN THE UNITED STATES AFTER THE REINSTATEMENT OF CAPITAL PUNISHMENT IN 1976. HE WAS EXECUTED IN OKLAHOMA AT THE AGE OF 22.

EARLY LIFE:

- BORN ON JANUARY 2, 1975.
- LITTLE IS PUBLICLY KNOWN ABOUT HIS UPBRINGING.
- HAD NO PRIOR CRIMINAL RECORD BEFORE THE MURDER.

THE CRIME:

- ON FEBRUARY 6, 1994, CARPENTER ENTERED A BAIT AND CONVENIENCE SHOP NEAR LAKE EUFAULA, OKLAHOMA.
- AFTER PLACING BAIT ITEMS NEAR THE COUNTER, HE
- FOLLOWED THE STORE OWNER, A.J. KELLEY, AND STABBED HIM IN THE NECK.
- HE FLED THE SCENE WITH APPROXIMATELY $37 WORTH OF GASOLINE.
- WITNESSES RECORDED HIS VEHICLE'S LICENSE PLATE, LEADING TO HIS ARREST ABOUT AN HOUR LATER.

ARREST & TRIAL:

- PLEADED NO CONTEST TO FIRST-DEGREE MURDER IN DECEMBER 1994.
- DECLINED TO PURSUE APPEALS, STATING HE SAW NO FUTURE IN PRISON AND PREFERRED EXECUTION.
- SENTENCED TO DEATH AND BECAME A RARE EXAMPLE OF A "VOLUNTEER" FOR EXECUTION.

EXECUTION:

- IN HIS FINAL STATEMENT, HE APOLOGIZED TO THE VICTIM'S FAMILY, WHICH THEY ACCEPTED, AND URGED OTHERS NOT TO FOLLOW HIS PATH.
- HIS PHYSICAL REACTION (INCLUDING PROLONGED SPASMS) DURING EXECUTION DREW ATTENTION, WHICH WAS ATTRIBUTED TO HIS YOUTH AND BUILD.

CONVICTED OF 1ST DEGREE MURDER, 1994.

SPENT 2 YEARS ON DEATH ROW.

EXECUTED BY LETHAL INJECTION ON MAY 8, 1997, AT AGE 22.

LAST MEAL–SCOTT CARPENTER

CRIME: MURDER
STATE: OKLAHOMA
YEAR: 1997
PUNISHMENT: LETHAL INJECTION

REQUESTED LAST MEAL:

BARBECUE BEEF RIBS, CORN ON THE COB, BAKED BEANS, POTATO SALAD, AND HOT ROLLS, SERVED WITH LEMONADE.

BARBECUE BEEF RIBS

INGREDIENTS:

- 6 X 300–350G|10–12 OZ BEEF RIBS
- 1 TABLESPOON BROWN SUGAR
- 2 TEASPOONS PAPRIKA
- 1 TEASPOON GARLIC POWDER
- 1 TEASPOON ONION POWDER
- 1/2 TEASPOON CUMIN POWDER
- 3/4 TEASPOON MUSTARD POWDER
- 1 TEASPOON COOKING SALT
- 1/2 TEASPOON BLACK PEPPER
- 2 GARLIC CLOVES, MINCED
- 120ML|1/2 CUP APPLE CIDER VINEGAR
- 350ML|1½ CUPS KETCHUP
- 105G|1/2 CUP BROWN SUGAR, LOOSELY PACKED
- 2 TEASPOON EACH: BLACK PEPPER, ONION POWDER, MUSTARD POWDER

- 1 TEASPOON CAYENNE PEPPER
- 1 TABLESPOON WORCESTERSHIRE SAUCE
- 475ML|2 CUPS WATER

BARBECUE BEEF RIBS

1. PREHEAT & SEASON
   - PREHEAT OVEN TO 160°C|320°F.
   - MIX RUB INGREDIENTS AND PRESS ONTO BEEF RIBS TO COAT ALL SIDES.

2. MAKE SAUCE & ADD RIBS
   - IN A BAKING PAN, MIX BBQ SAUCE INGREDIENTS WITH WATER.
   - ADD RIBS MEAT-SIDE DOWN AND TURN TO COAT.

3. BAKE COVERED
   - COVER TIGHTLY WITH FOIL AND BAKE FOR 3½ HOURS.

4. BAKE UNCOVERED
   - REMOVE FOIL, TURN RIBS, SPOON OVER SAUCE, AND BAKE UNCOVERED FOR 30 MINUTES UNTIL STICKY.

5. SERVE
   - REMOVE RIBS CAREFULLY (THEY WILL BE VERY TENDER), STIR SAUCE, SPOON OVER RIBS, AND SERVE HOT.

BIOGRAPHY-JOHN DEERING

LAST WORDS:

"GOOD-BYE AND GOOD LUCK! OKAY, LET IT GO."

BORN:	09/1898
DIED:	10/31/1938 (AGED 40)
CONVICTIONS:	FIRST-DEGREE MURDER
PENALTY:	DEATH

JOHN W. DEERING (1898-1938) WAS A CONVICTED MURDERER WHO BECAME THE SUBJECT OF A PIONEERING MEDICAL EXPERIMENT DURING HIS EXECUTION. HE WAS EXECUTED BY FIRING SQUAD IN UTAH, AGE 40.

EARLY LIFE:

- BORN SEPTEMBER 1898 IN CHICAGO, ILLINOIS.
- EXPERIENCED A TUMULTUOUS CHILDHOOD MARKED BY NEGLECT.
- COMMITTED TO A REFORMATORY FROM AGES 13 TO 18.
- SERVED TIME IN SAN QUENTIN AND FOLSOM STATE PRISONS FOR VARIOUS OFFENSES.

THE CRIME:

- IN MAY 1938, DEERING MURDERED OLIVER R. MEREDITH JR. DURING A ROBBERY IN SALT LAKE CITY.
- CAPTURED IN MICHIGAN, HE CONFESSED TO THE MURDER TO AVOID A 15-YEAR SENTENCE IN MICHIGAN.

EXECUTION:

- EXECUTED BY FIRING SQUAD ON OCTOBER 31, 1938, AT SUGAR HOUSE PRISON IN SALT LAKE CITY.
- VOLUNTEERED TO HAVE HIS HEART MONITORED VIA ELECTROCARDIOGRAM DURING THE EXECUTION.
- HEART RATE INCREASED FROM 72 TO 180 BEATS PER MINUTE UPON BEING STRAPPED INTO THE CHAIR.
- HEART STOPPED 15.6 SECONDS AFTER BEING SHOT; CONTINUED BREATHING FOR NEARLY A MINUTE BEFORE BEING PRONOUNCED DEAD.

CONVICTED OF MURDER, 1938.

SPENT 3 MONTHS ON DEATH ROW.

EXECUTED BY FIRING SQUAD IN UTAH AT AGE 40.

CRIME: MURDER
STATE: UTAH
YEAR: 1938
PUNISHMENT: FIRING SQUAD

REQUESTED LAST MEAL:

PHEASANT.

ROAST PHEASANT

INGREDIENTS:

- 2 SPRIGS ROSEMARY, LEAVES STRIPPED AND CHOPPED
- 1 TABLESPOON FRESH THYME, CHOPPED
- 1 CUP OLIVE OIL
- 1 WHOLE PHEASANT, CLEANED
- SALT AND PEPPER TO TASTE

METHOD

ROAST PHEASANT

1. PREHEAT & SEASON

- PREHEAT OVEN TO 120°C|250°F.
- MIX ROSEMARY AND THYME INTO OLIVE OIL.
- RUB PHEASANT INSIDE AND OUT WITH SALT AND PEPPER.

2. PREP FOR ROASTING

- PLACE PHEASANT IN A SMALL ROASTING PAN AND POUR HERB OIL OVER THE TOP.

3. BAKE & BASTE

- BAKE UNCOVERED FOR 1 HOUR.
- THEN COVER WITH FOIL AND CONTINUE BAKING FOR ABOUT 1 MORE HOUR, UNTIL INTERNAL TEMP REACHES 82°C| 180°F.
- BASTE WITH PAN JUICES EVERY 30 MINUTES.

5. REST & SERVE

- REMOVE FROM OVEN, COVER WITH FOIL, AND LET REST FOR 10 MINUTES BEFORE SLICING.
- SERVE AND ENJOY.

LAST MEAL-CHARLES WALKER

Charles Walker

CRIME: MURDER
STATE: ILLINOIS
YEAR: 1990
PUNISHMENT: LETHAL INJECTION

REQUESTED LAST MEAL:

FRIED WILD RABBIT, BISCUITS, BLACKBERRY PIE.

FRIED WILD RABBIT

INGREDIENTS:

- 710ML|3 CUPS BUTTERMILK
- 2 TEASPOONS KOSHER SALT
- 1/2 TEASPOON MUSTARD POWDER
- 1/2 TEASPOON PAPRIKA
- 1/4 TEASPOON FRESHLY GROUND BLACK PEPPER
- 1/4 TEASPOON GARLIC POWDER
- 1/4 TEASPOON ONION POWDER
- 8 SPRIGS FRESH THYME, PICKED
- 2 SPRIGS FRESH ROSEMARY, PICKED AND CHOPPED
- 1 RABBIT, BROKEN DOWN INTO 2 FRONT LEGS, 2 HIND QUARTERS, 1 SADDLE CUT CUT IN HALF CROSSWISE
- 260G|2 CUPS ALL-PURPOSE FLOUR

LAST MEAL

- 1 TABLESPOON KOSHER SALT
- 1/2 TEASPOON FRESHLY GROUND BLACK PEPPER
- 1L | 4 CUPS VEGETABLE OIL, FOR FRYING

FRIED WILD RABBIT

1. BRINE THE RABBIT

- IN A LARGE BOWL, WHISK TOGETHER:
- BUTTERMILK, SALT, MUSTARD POWDER, PAPRIKA, PEPPER, GARLIC POWDER, ONION POWDER, ROSEMARY, AND THYME.
- ADD RABBIT PIECES AND COAT WELL.
- TRANSFER TO A ZIP-TOP BAG AND REFRIGERATE FOR 8-12 HOURS, FLIPPING OCCASIONALLY.

2. DREDGE THE RABBIT

- PREHEAT OVEN TO 95°C|200°F. SET A WIRE RACK OVER A BAKING SHEET.
- IN A BOWL, WHISK TOGETHER FLOUR, SALT, AND PEPPER.
- REMOVE RABBIT FROM BRINE ONE PIECE AT A TIME. LET EXCESS DRIP OFF.
- COAT IN FLOUR MIXTURE, PRESSING TO STICK. PLACE ON RACK.
- REPEAT WITH ALL PIECES AND LET REST 15 MINUTES.

3. FRY THE RABBIT

- LINE ANOTHER BAKING SHEET WITH PAPER TOWELS AND TOP WITH A CLEAN RACK.
- HEAT OIL IN A LARGE SKILLET OR WOK TO 175°C|350°F.
- FRY HALF THE RABBIT UNTIL GOLDEN, ABOUT 8-10 MINUTES.
- FLIP AND FRY OTHER SIDE UNTIL COOKED THROUGH (70°C|160°F INSIDE), ABOUT 7 MINUTES.
- TRANSFER TO CLEAN RACK, LIGHTLY SALT, AND KEEP WARM IN OVEN.
- REPEAT WITH REMAINING RABBIT.

4. REST & SERVE

- LET RABBIT REST 5 MINUTES BEFORE SERVING.
- ENJOY HOT AND CRISPY!

CRIME: MURDER AND RAPE
STATE: TEXAS
YEAR: 2011
PUNISHMENT: LETHAL INJECTION

REQUESTED LAST MEAL:

FRIED CHICKEN, PICO DE GALLO, TACOS, TWO COKES, AND A BOWL OF FRIED OKRA

PICO DE GALLO

INGREDIENTS:

- 150G|1 CUP FINELY CHOPPED WHITE ONION
- 1 MEDIUM JALAPEÑO, RIBS AND SEEDS REMOVED, FINELY CHOPPED
- 60ML|1/4 CUP LIME JUICE
- 3/4 TEASPOON FINE SEA SALT, MORE TO TASTE
- 680G|1½ LB RIPE RED TOMATOES, CHOPPED
- 9G|1/2 CUP FRESH CILANTRO, FINELY CHOPPED

LAST MEAL

METHOD

PICO DE GALLO

1. MARINATE THE BASE
   - ADD CHOPPED ONION, JALAPEÑO, LIME JUICE, AND SALT TO A MEDIUM SERVING BOWL.
   - LET SIT FOR 5 MINUTES TO MARINATE WHILE YOU PREP THE OTHER INGREDIENTS.

2. ADD FRESH INGREDIENTS
   - CHOP TOMATOES AND CILANTRO, THEN ADD THEM TO THE BOWL.
   - STIR TO COMBINE. TASTE AND ADJUST SALT IF NEEDED.

3. LET FLAVORS DEVELOP
   - FOR BEST TASTE, LET THE MIXTURE MARINATE FOR 15 MINUTES OR LONGER IN THE FRIDGE.
   - THE FLAVORS INTENSIFY OVER TIME.

4. SERVE OR STORE
   - SERVE AS A DIP OR WITH A SLOTTED SPOON TO AVOID TOO MUCH LIQUID.
   - COVER AND STORE IN THE FRIDGE FOR UP TO 4 DAYS.

Last words

"I HAVE HURT A LOT OF PEOPLE. LET THIS BE FINAL AND BE DONE. I TAKE THE FULL BLAME FOR THIS. I AM SORRY AND FORGIVE ME, I AM TRULY SORRY. I AM SORRY FOR THE VICTIM'S FAMILY AND WHAT I HAD DID, MAY THEY FORGIVE ME. I DON'T KNOW IF YOU BELIEVE ME. ONE MORE THING, VIVA MEXICO. VIVA MEXICO."

BIOGRAPHY-TIMOTHY MCVEIGH

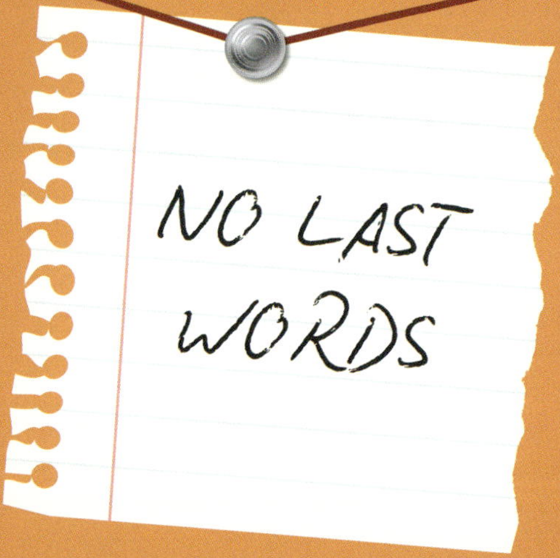

BORN:	04/23/1968
DIED:	06/11/2001 (AGED 33)
CONVICTIONS:	FIRST-DEGREE MURDER OF A FEDERAL EMPLOYEE (8 COUNTS). USE OF A WEAPON OF MASS DESTRUCTION RESULTING IN DEATH. CONSPIRACY TO USE A WEAPON OF MASS DESTRUCTION RESULTING IN DEATH. DESTRUCTION BY EXPLOSIVES RESULTING IN DEATH.
PENALTY:	DEATH

TIMOTHY JAMES MCVEIGH (1968-2001) WAS A DOMESTIC TERRORIST RESPONSIBLE FOR THE 1995 OKLAHOMA CITY BOMBING, THE DEADLIEST ACT OF DOMESTIC TERRORISM IN U.S. HISTORY AT THE TIME. HE WAS EXECUTED FOR KILLING 168 PEOPLE AND INJURING HUNDREDS MORE.

EARLY LIFE:

- BORN ON APRIL 23, 1968, IN LOCKPORT, NEW YORK.
- GREW UP IN A WORKING-CLASS FAMILY.
- BECAME INTERESTED IN GUNS AND SURVIVALISM AT A YOUNG AGE.
- SERVED IN THE U.S. ARMY DURING THE GULF WAR, WHERE HE EARNED A BRONZE STAR AND GAINED EXPERTISE IN EXPLOSIVES.

THE CRIME:

- ON APRIL 19, 1995, MCVEIGH DETONATED A TRUCK BOMB OUTSIDE THE ALFRED P. MURRAH FEDERAL BUILDING IN OKLAHOMA CITY.
- THE BOMBING KILLED 168 PEOPLE, INCLUDING 19 CHILDREN, AND INJURED OVER 600.
- THE DATE WAS CHOSEN TO COINCIDE WITH THE SECOND ANNIVERSARY OF THE WACO SIEGE, WHICH MCVEIGH VIEWED AS GOVERNMENT TYRANNY.
- HE ACTED OUT OF ANTI-GOVERNMENT MOTIVES, HOPING TO SPARK A REVOLUTION.

ARREST AND TRIAL:

- ARRESTED JUST 90 MINUTES AFTER THE BOMBING DURING A ROUTINE TRAFFIC STOP FOR A MISSING LICENSE PLATE.
- EVIDENCE, INCLUDING RECEIPTS AND EYEWITNESS ACCOUNTS, LINKED HIM TO THE RYDER TRUCK USED IN THE BOMBING.
- TRIED IN FEDERAL COURT AND FOUND GUILTY ON ALL COUNTS IN 1997.
- SENTENCED TO DEATH; NEVER SHOWED REMORSE AND CALLED THE DEATHS “COLLATERAL DAMAGE.”

EXECUTION:

- HIS EXECUTION WAS WITNESSED BY OVER 200 PEOPLE VIA CLOSED-CIRCUIT BROADCAST.

CONVICTED IN 1997.

SPENT ALMOST 4 YEARS ON DEATH ROW.

EXECUTED BY LETHAL INJECTION ON JUNE 11, 2001, AGE 33.

LAST MEAL–TIMOTHY MCVEIGH

Timothy McVeigh

CRIME: DOMESTIC TERRORISM
STATE: FEDERAL GOVERNMENT
YEAR: 2001
PUNISHMENT: LETHAL INJECTION

REQUESTED LAST MEAL:

TWO PINTS OF MINT CHOCOLATE CHIP ICE CREAM.

MINT ICE CREAM

INGREDIENTS:

- 475ML|2 CUPS
- WHIPPING CREAM
- 400ML|14 OZ SWEETENED CONDENSED MILK
- 1 TSP PEPPERMINT EXTRACT
- 3-6 DROPS GREEN FOOD COLORING
- 170G|1 CUP CHOPPED UP CHOCOLATE

LAST MEAL

MINT ICE CREAM

1. WHIP THE CREAM
   - IN A LARGE BOWL, WHIP HEAVY CREAM ON HIGH SPEED UNTIL STIFF PEAKS FORM.

2. MIX FLAVOR BASE
   - IN ANOTHER BOWL, COMBINE CONDENSED MILK, PEPPERMINT EXTRACT, AND FOOD COLORING.

3. COMBINE & FOLD
   - POUR CONDENSED MILK MIXTURE AND CHOPPED CHOCOLATE INTO WHIPPED CREAM.
   - FOLD GENTLY UNTIL EVENLY COMBINED.

4. FREEZE
   - TRANSFER MIXTURE TO A 3L|3-QUART PAN. COVER TIGHTLY WITH PLASTIC WRAP.
   - FREEZE FOR AT LEAST 6 HOURS OR OVERNIGHT.

5. SERVE
   - SCOOP AND ENJOY!

BIOGRAPHY-ODELL BARNES JR.

"I'D LIKE TO SEND GREAT LOVE TO ALL MY FAMILY MEMBERS, MY SUPPORTERS, MY ATTORNEYS. THEY HAVE ALL SUPPORTED ME THROUGHOUT THIS. I THANK YOU FOR PROVING MY INNOCENCE, ALTHOUGH IT HAS NOT BEEN ACKNOWLEDGED BY THE COURTS. MAY YOU CONTINUE IN THE STRUGGLE AND MAY YOU CHANGE ALL THAT'S BEING DONE HERE TODAY AND IN THE PAST. LIFE HAS NOT BEEN GOOD TO ME, BUT I BELIEVE THAT NOW, AFTER MEETING SO MANY PEOPLE WHO SUPPORT ME IN THIS, THAT ALL THINGS WILL COME TO AN END, AND MAY THIS BE FRUIT OF BETTER JUDGMENTS FOR THE FUTURE. THAT'S ALL I HAVE TO SAY."

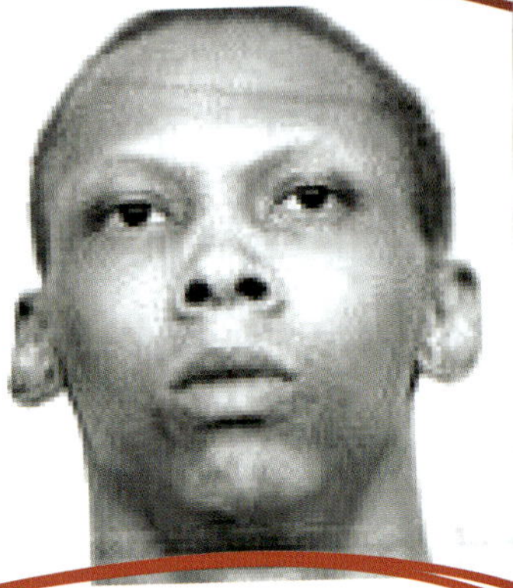

Odell Barnes JR

Last words

REQUESTED LAST MEAL: JUSTICE, EQUALITY, WORLD PEACE.

BORN:	03/22/1968
DIED:	03/01/2000 (AGED 31)
CONVICTIONS:	MURDER, AGGRAVATED SEXUAL ASSAULT
PENALTY:	DEATH

ODELL BARNES JR. (1968-2000) WAS A TEXAS MAN CONVICTED OF MURDER AND EXECUTED IN 2000. HIS CASE DREW INTERNATIONAL ATTENTION AND BECAME CONTROVERSIAL DUE TO SERIOUS CONCERNS ABOUT THE FAIRNESS OF HIS TRIAL, QUALITY OF EVIDENCE, AND POSSIBLE POLICE MISCONDUCT. MANY CRITICS ARGUED HE MAY HAVE BEEN WRONGFULLY CONVICTED.

EARLY LIFE:

- BORN IN WICHITA COUNTY, TEXAS, IN 1968.
- PRIOR TO THE MURDER CHARGE, HAD MINOR RUN-INS WITH THE LAW BUT NO HISTORY OF VIOLENT CRIME.

THE CRIME:

- IN 1989, HELEN BASS, A WHITE WOMAN, WAS FOUND RAPED, BEATEN, AND FATALLY SHOT IN HER HOME.
- ODELL BARNES JR., A BLACK MAN, WAS ARRESTED BASED ON: A WITNESS WHO CLAIMED TO HAVE SEEN HIM NEAR THE VICTIM'S HOUSE, AND FINGERPRINTS IN HER HOME.

TRAIL AND CONVICTION:

- BARNES WAS CONVICTED AND SENTENCED TO DEATH.
- PROSECUTORS CLAIMED DNA AND PHYSICAL EVIDENCE (LIKE BLOOD AND SEMEN) TIED HIM TO THE CRIME SCENE.
- HIS TRIAL DEFENSE WAS SEVERELY UNDER-RESOURCED, WITH LITTLE EXPERT TESTIMONY OR INVESTIGATION.

CONTROVERSY AND APPEALS:

- AS HIS EXECUTION NEARED, INTERNATIONAL HUMAN RIGHTS GROUPS TOOK UP HIS CASE DUE TO: DNA EVIDENCE INCONSISTENCIES, UNCLEAR TIMELINE OF DEATH VS. ALIBI,POSSIBLE CONTAMINATION OR MISHANDLING OF FORENSIC EVIDENCE, ALLEGATIONS THAT BARNES'S CONFESSION WAS COERCED OR FABRICATED.
- NEW FORENSIC EXPERTS ARGUED THE CASE AGAINST HIM WAS DEEPLY FLAWED AND POSSIBLY FABRICATED.

EXECUTION:

- DESPITE THE APPEALS AND CONTROVERSY, BARNES WAS EXECUTED BY LETHAL INJECTION.
- HIS LAST WORDS WERE A PLEA FOR PEACE AND RECONCILIATION, ACKNOWLEDGING HIS FAMILY AND SUPPORTERS.

CONVICTED IN 1991.

SPENT ALMOST 9 YEARS ON DEATH ROW.

EXECUTED BY LETHAL INJECTION ON MARCH 1, 2000, IN TEXAS.

BIOGRAPHY–TED BUNDY

Last words:

"JIM AND FRED, I'D LIKE YOU TO GIVE MY LOVE TO MY FAMILY AND FRIENDS"

AKA:	THE LADY KILLER
BORN:	11/24/1946
DIED:	01/24/1982 (AGED 42)
CONVICTIONS:	FIRST-DEGREE MURDER (3 COUNTS). ATTEMPTED FIRST-DEGREE MURDER (3 COUNTS). AGGRAVATED KIDNAP.
PENALTY:	3 DEATH SENTENCES

THEODORE ROBERT BUNDY (1946–1989) WAS A SERIAL KILLER, RAPIST, AND NECROPHILE WHO MURDERED NUMEROUS YOUNG WOMEN DURING THE 1970S. HE IS ONE OF THE MOST NOTORIOUS AND STUDIED SERIAL KILLERS IN U.S. HISTORY, KNOWN FOR HIS DECEPTIVE CHARM AND EXTREME BRUTALITY.

EARLY LIFE:

- BORN ON NOVEMBER 24, 1946, IN BURLINGTON, VERMONT.
- RAISED BELIEVING HIS MOTHER WAS HIS SISTER AND HIS GRANDPARENTS WERE HIS PARENTS.
- STUDIED PSYCHOLOGY AT THE UNIVERSITY OF WASHINGTON.
- LATER ATTENDED LAW SCHOOL BUT NEVER EARNED A DEGREE.

THE CRIMES:

- BEGAN ABDUCTING AND MURDERING YOUNG WOMEN IN 1974.
- LURED VICTIMS BY FEIGNING INJURY OR IMPERSONATING AUTHORITY FIGURES.
- ATTACKED, RAPED, AND MURDERED WOMEN ACROSS AT LEAST SEVEN STATES, OFTEN REVISITING BODIES AND ENGAGING IN NECROPHILIA.
- COMMITTED HIS MOST NOTORIOUS ATTACKS IN 1978 AT THE CHI OMEGA SORORITY HOUSE IN FLORIDA.
- ESTIMATED TO HAVE KILLED AT LEAST 30 WOMEN, THOUGH THE ACTUAL NUMBER MAY BE HIGHER.

ARREST AND TRIALS:

- FIRST ARRESTED IN UTAH IN 1975; LINKED TO MULTIPLE DISAPPEARANCES.
- ESCAPED CUSTODY TWICE IN 1977, FLEEING TO FLORIDA AND COMMITTING ADDITIONAL MURDERS.
- CAPTURED IN FEBRUARY 1978 AND TRIED FOR THE CHI OMEGA MURDERS.
- REPRESENTED HIMSELF DURING TRIAL, USING THE COURTROOM AS A STAGE FOR MANIPULATION.
- CONVICTED AND SENTENCED TO DEATH IN 1979 AND AGAIN IN 1980 FOR SEPARATE MURDERS.

EXECUTION:

- BEFORE HIS EXECUTION, CONFESSED TO 30 MURDERS BUT REFUSED TO GIVE FULL DETAILS.
- CROWDS CHEERED AS THE EXECUTION TOOK PLACE.

CONVICTED IN 1979 AND AGAIN 1980.

SPENT 9 YEARS ON DEATH ROW.

EXECUTED BY ELECTRIC CHAIR ON JANUARY 24, 1989, IN FLORIDA.

LAST MEAL–TED BUNDY

AKA: LADY KILLER
CRIME: SERIAL MURDER
STATE: FLORIDA
YEAR: 1989
PUNISHMENT: ELECTRIC CHAIR

REQUESTED LAST MEAL:

DECLINED A SPECIAL MEAL SO WAS GIVEN (BUT DID NOT EAT) THE TRADITIONAL STEAK (MEDIUM-RARE), EGGS (OVER EASY), HASHBROWNS, TOAST, MILK, COFFEE, JUICE, BUTTER, AND JELLY

MEDIUM-RARE STEAK

INGREDIENTS:

- 900G|2 LBS NEW YORK STRIP STEAK
- 1 TABLESPOON VEGETABLE OIL
- 2 TEASPOON SALT
- 1½ TEASPOON BLACK PEPPER
- 3 TABLESPOONS UNSALTED BUTTER
- 6 CLOVES GARLIC, PEELED AND QUARTERED
- 2 SPRIGS FRESH ROSEMARY
- 2-3 SPRIGS FRESH THYME
- 1 SPRIG FRESH SAGE

MEDIUM-RARE STEAK

1. SEASON THE STEAKS

- PAT STEAKS DRY WITH PAPER TOWELS.
- SEASON GENEROUSLY WITH SALT AND PEPPER ON BOTH SIDES.

2. SEAR THE STEAKS

- HEAT ½-1 TBSP VEGETABLE OIL IN A HOT CAST IRON SKILLET OVER MEDIUM-HIGH.
- ADD STEAKS AND SEAR FOR 3-4 MINUTES PER SIDE UNTIL A BROWN CRUST FORMS.
- USE TONGS TO SEAR THE EDGES AND RENDER FAT (1-2 MINUTES EACH SIDE).

3. BUTTER BASTE

- REDUCE HEAT TO MEDIUM. ADD BUTTER, GARLIC, AND HERBS.
- SPOON HOT BUTTER OVER STEAKS CONTINUOUSLY UNTIL THEY'RE 10°F BELOW DESIRED TEMP.

4. REST & SLICE

- TRANSFER STEAKS TO A CUTTING BOARD. COVER LOOSELY WITH FOIL AND REST 10 MINUTES.
- SLICE INTO ½-1 INCH STRIPS. SERVE WITH EXTRA BUTTER SAUCE.MINUTES UNTIL STICKY.

BIOGRAPHY-THOMAS MARTIN THOMPSON

Last words:

"FOR 17 YEARS THE AG HAS BEEN PURSUING THE WRONG MAN. IN TIME HE WILL COME TO KNOW THIS. I DON'T WANT ANYONE TO AVENGE MY DEATH. INSTEAD I WANT YOU TO STOP KILLING PEOPLE. GOD BLESS."

Thomas Martin Thompson

BORN:	03/20/1955
DIED:	07/14/1998 (AGED 43)
CONVICTIONS:	FIRST-DEGREE MURDER WITH SPECIAL CIRCUMSTANCES. FORCIBLE RAPE.
PENALTY:	DEATH

THOMAS MARTIN THOMPSON (1955-1998) WAS EXECUTED IN CALIFORNIA FOR THE 1981 RAPE AND MURDER OF GINGER FLEISCHLI. HIS CASE BECAME ONE OF THE MOST CONTROVERSIAL IN THE STATE'S MODERN DEATH PENALTY HISTORY, RAISING SERIOUS QUESTIONS ABOUT EVIDENCE RELIABILITY AND THE FAIRNESS OF HIS TRIAL.

EARLY LIFE:

- BORN MARCH 20, 1955, IN CHICAGO; RAISED IN NEW YORK AND LATER IN ORANGE COUNTY, CALIFORNIA.
- ENLISTED IN THE U.S. ARMY, RECEIVING AN HONORABLE DISCHARGE.

THE CRIME:

- ON SEPTEMBER 11, 1981, THOMPSON INVITED 20-YEAR-OLD GINGER FLEISCHLI TO SPEND THE EVENING WITH HIM AND FRIENDS IN LAGUNA BEACH.
- DAYS LATER, HER BODY WAS FOUND BURIED IN A FIELD – SHE HAD BEEN RAPED AND STABBED.
- THOMPSON WAS LINKED TO THE CRIME THROUGH PHYSICAL EVIDENCE, AND A FORMER ROOMMATE, DAVID LEITCH, WAS ALSO IMPLICATED.

ARREST AND TRIAL:

- IN NOVEMBER 1983, THOMPSON WAS CONVICTED OF FIRST-DEGREE MURDER AND RAPE WITH SPECIAL CIRCUMSTANCES, AND SENTENCED TO DEATH.
- THE PROSECUTION'S CASE RELIED HEAVILY ON JAILHOUSE INFORMANTS AND FORENSIC TESTIMONY.
- THE CALIFORNIA SUPREME COURT UPHELD THE CONVICTION AND SENTENCE IN 1988.

APPEALS AND CONTROVERSY:

- A FEDERAL COURT VACATED THE DEATH SENTENCE IN 1995, CITING INEFFECTIVE DEFENSE COUNSEL.
- A NINTH CIRCUIT PANEL THEN REINSTATED IT IN 1996.
- IN 1997, THE FULL NINTH CIRCUIT ISSUED A STAY OF EXECUTION, CITING SERIOUS DOUBTS ABOUT THOMPSON'S GUILT AND TRIAL FAIRNESS.
- THE U.S. SUPREME COURT OVERTURNED THE STAY.
- A FEDERAL JUDGE LATER STATED THOMPSON WAS "LIKELY INNOCENT," CRITICIZING THE LIMITED ABILITY OF COURTS TO CORRECT INJUSTICES.

CONVICTED IN 1983.

SPENT 13 YEARS ON DEATH ROW.

EXECUTED BY LETHAL INJECTION ON JULY 14, 1998, AGE 43.

CRIME: SERIAL MURDER
STATE: CALIFORNIA
YEAR: 1998
PUNISHMENT: LETHAL INJECTION

REQUESTED LAST MEAL:

ALASKAN KING CRAB WITH MELTED BUTTER, SPINACH SALAD, PORK FRIED RICE, MANDARIN-STYLE SPARE RIBS, A HOT FUDGE SUNDAE, AND A SIX-PACK OF COCA-COLA.

MANDARIN-STYLE SPARE RIBS

INGREDIENTS:

- 1.2KG|2.7 LBS PORK SPARE RIBS
- 1 TEASPOON SESAME SEED OIL
- 2 TABLESPOONS GRATED GINGER
- 3 TABLESPOONS SOY SAUCE
- 2 TABLESPOONS BLACK VINEGAR
- 2 TABLESPOONS MIRIN
- 475-590ML|2-2½ CUPS MANDARIN ORANGE JUICE
- SALT TO TASTE
- SUGAR (OPTIONAL)
- 250G|1 CUP MANDARIN ORANGE SEGMENTS
- 50G|1/2 CUP SLICED SCALLIONS

LAST MEAL

METHOD

MANDARIN-STYLE SPARE RIBS

1. SEAR THE RIBS
   - PAT RIBS DRY WITH A KITCHEN TOWEL.
   - HEAT SESAME SEED OIL IN A WIDE SHALLOW PAN.
   - ADD RIBS IN A SINGLE LAYER AND SEAR ON ALL SIDES UNTIL BROWNED.

2. ADD SEASONINGS
   - SPRINKLE GRATED GINGER OVER RIBS.
   - POUR IN SOY SAUCE, BLACK VINEGAR, AND MIRIN.
   - SWIRL TO MIX, BRING TO A BOIL, AND COOK UNCOVERED FOR 5 MINUTES, TURNING OCCASIONALLY.

3. BRAISE THE RIBS
   - ADD ORANGE JUICE AND SALT.
   - BRING TO A BOIL, THEN LOWER HEAT, COVER, AND SIMMER FOR ABOUT 1 HOUR, UNTIL TENDER.
   - TASTE AND ADJUST SEASONING WITH SALT OR SUGAR IF NEEDED.

4. GLAZE AND FINISH
   - UNCOVER, INCREASE HEAT, AND COOK UNTIL SAUCE IS STICKY AND REDUCED.
   - TURN RIBS TO CARAMELIZE ON ALL SIDES.

5. SERVE
   - TRANSFER RIBS TO A PLATE.
   - DRIZZLE WITH SAUCE AND GARNISH WITH MANDARIN ORANGE SEGMENTS AND SLICED SCALLIONS.
   - SERVE HOT.

BIOGRAPHY-KELLY RENEE GISSENDANER

SHE CRIED, PRAYED, SANG 'AMAZING GRACE', AND SAID:

"AND I LOVE YOU SALLY. AND I LOVE YOU SUSAN. YOU LET MY KIDS KNOW I WENT OUT SINGING AMAZING GRACE. AND TELL THE GISSENDANER FAMILY I AM SO SORRY. THAT AMAZING MAN LOST HIS LIFE BECAUSE OF ME AND IF I COULD TAKE IT BACK, IF THIS WOULD CHANGE IT, I WOULD HAVE DONE IT A LONG TIME AGO. BUT IT'S NOT. AND I JUST HOPE THEY CAN FIND PEACE. AND I HOPE THEY FIND SOME HAPPINESS. GOD BLESS YOU."

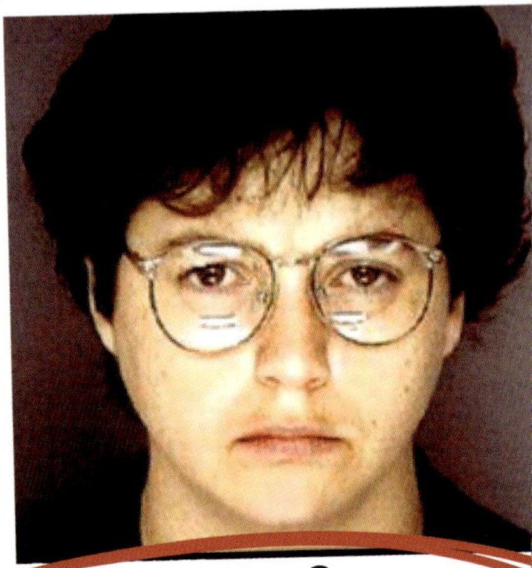

Kelly Renee Gissendaner

Last words

BORN:	03/08/1968
DIED:	09/30/2015 (AGED 47)
CONVICTIONS:	MALICE MURDER
PENALTY:	DEATH

KELLY RENEE GISSENDANER (1968-2015) WAS EXECUTED IN GEORGIA FOR ORCHESTRATING THE 1997 MURDER OF HER HUSBAND. SHE WAS THE FIRST WOMAN EXECUTED IN THE STATE IN 70 YEARS AND THE ONLY WOMAN ON GEORGIA'S DEATH ROW AT THE TIME.

EARLY LIFE:

- BORN ON MARCH 8, 1968, IN LAWRENCEVILLE, GEORGIA.
- EXPERIENCED SEXUAL ABUSE AS A CHILD, MOLESTED BY HER STEPFATHER AND OTHERS DURING HER UPBRINGING.
- MARRIED JEFF BANKS IN 1987; DIVORCED THE SAME YEAR.
- MARRIED DOUGLAS GISSENDANER IN 1989; THE COUPLE HAD THREE CHILDREN BEFORE DIVORCING IN 1993.THEY REMARRIED IN 1995.

THE CRIME:

- IN FEBRUARY 1997, GISSENDANER CONSPIRED WITH HER LOVER, GREGORY OWEN, TO MURDER HER HUSBAND, DOUGLAS GISSENDANER.
- OWEN AMBUSHED DOUGLAS, FORCED HIM INTO HIS OWN CAR, FATALLY STABBED HIM, AND SET THE CAR ON FIRE.
- GISSENDANER WAS CONVICTED OF MALICE MURDER IN 1998.

PRISON LIFE AND THEOLOGY:

- WHILE ON DEATH ROW, GISSENDANER UNDERWENT A PROFOUND PERSONAL TRANSFORMATION.
- SHE STUDIED THEOLOGY EXTENSIVELY AND BECAME A CHRISTIAN MINISTER.
- GISSENDANER COUNSELED AND MENTORED OTHER INMATES, BECOMING A SPIRITUAL LEADER WITHIN THE PRISON.
- HER FAITH AND MINISTRY EFFORTS BROUGHT NATIONAL ATTENTION AND SPARKED DEBATE ABOUT REDEMPTION AND THE DEATH PENALTY.

EXECUTION:

- EXECUTION WAS DELAYED MULTIPLE TIMES DUE TO WEATHER AND ISSUES WITH LETHAL INJECTION DRUGS.

CONVICTED IN 1998.

SPENT 17 YEARS ON DEATH ROW.

EXECUTED BY LETHAL INJECTION ON SEPTEMBER 30, 2015,AGE 47.

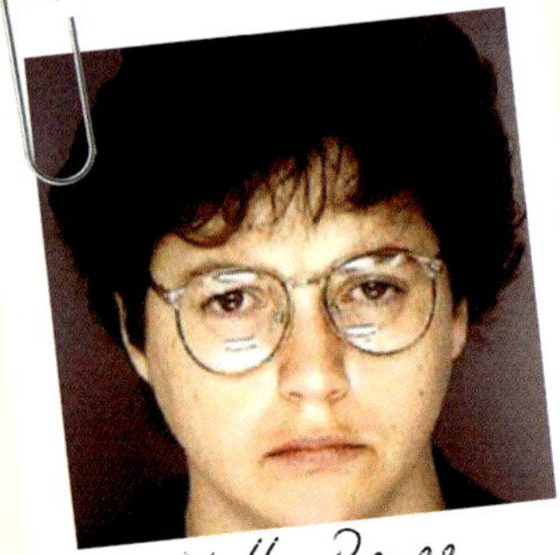

Kelly Renee Gissendaner

CRIME: SERIAL MURDER
STATE: GEORGIA
YEAR: 2015
PUNISHMENT: LETHAL INJECTION

REQUESTED LAST MEAL:

CHEESE DIP WITH CHIPS, TEXAS NACHOS WITH FAJITA MEAT, AND DIET FROSTED LEMONADE.

CHEESE DIP WITH CHIPS

INGREDIENTS:

- 2 TABLESPOONS BUTTER
- 2 TABLESPOONS FLOUR
- 240ML|1 CUP WHOLE MILK
- 170G|6 OZ MEDIUM CHEDDAR, SHREDDED
- 1/4 TEASPOON SALT
- 1/4 TEASPOON CHILI POWDER

LAST MEAL

METHOD

CHEESE DIP WITH CHIPS

1. MAKE THE ROUX
   - ADD BUTTER AND FLOUR TO A SMALL SAUCEPAN.
   - COOK AND WHISK OVER MEDIUM HEAT UNTIL BUBBLY AND FOAMY, ABOUT 1 MINUTE.

2. ADD MILK & THICKEN
   - WHISK IN MILK AND TURN UP THE HEAT SLIGHTLY.
   - BRING TO A SIMMER WHILE WHISKING UNTIL SAUCE THICKENS AND COATS A SPOON.

3. ADD CHEESE
   - TURN OFF HEAT. STIR IN SHREDDED CHEDDAR, A HANDFUL AT A TIME, UNTIL MELTED.
   - (IF NEEDED, USE LOW HEAT TO HELP MELT – DO NOT OVERHEAT.)

4. SEASON & ADJUST
   - STIR IN SALT AND CHILI POWDER.
   - TASTE AND ADJUST SEASONING.
   - IF TOO THICK, WHISK IN A SPLASH OF MILK.

5. SERVE WITH CHIPS
   - SERVE WITH CHIPS AND ENJOY.

CRIME: MURDER AND KIDNAPPING
STATE: LOUISIANA
YEAR: 2010
PUNISHMENT: LETHAL INJECTION

REQUESTED LAST MEAL:

FRIED SAC-À-LAIT FISH, TOPPED WITH CRAWFISH ÉTOUFFÉE, A PEANUT BUTTER AND APPLE JELLY SANDWICH, AND CHOCOLATE CHIP COOKIES

FRIED SAC-À-LAIT FISH

INGREDIENTS:

- WHOLE SAC-À-LAIT (SCALED, GUTTED, AND DE-HEADED)
- CAJUN SEASONING
- 1 EGG
- 240ML|1 CUP BUTTERMILK
- DRY FISH BATTER (OR EQUAL PARTS FLOUR AND CORNMEAL)

FRIED SAC-À-LAIT

1. PREPARE THE FISH

- WASH A SCALED, GUTTED, AND DE-HEADED WHOLE FISH INSIDE AND OUT.
- OPTIONALLY, TRIM FINS WITH KITCHEN SHEARS.
- MAKE SHALLOW DIAGONAL SLITS ON BOTH SIDES OF EACH FISH.

2. SEASON AND MARINATE

- SEASON FISH GENEROUSLY INSIDE AND OUT WITH CAJUN SEASONING (STORE-BOUGHT OR HOMEMADE).
- PLACE IN A LARGE ZIP-TOP BAG AND REFRIGERATE FOR A FEW HOURS.

3. PREP BATTER STATIONS

- IN A PAN, MIX 1 BEATEN EGG WITH ABOUT 130ML|1 CUP MILK OR BUTTERMILK.
- OPTIONAL: ADD A DASH OF HOT SAUCE FOR EXTRA SPICE.
- ADD FISH-FRY MIX (OR EQUAL PARTS FLOUR AND CORNMEAL) TO A LARGE ZIP-TOP BAG.

4. HEAT OIL

- HEAT VEGETABLE OR PEANUT OIL IN A LARGE PAN TO 190°C|375°F.
- USE A THERMOMETER TO MAINTAIN OIL TEMP BETWEEN 175-190°C|350-375°F, AIMING FOR 180°C|360°F.

5. BATTER AND FRY

- DIP 2-3 FISH AT A TIME IN EGG/MILK MIXTURE, SHAKE OFF EXCESS.
- ADD TO FISH-FRY BAG, SEAL, AND SHAKE TO COAT EVENLY.
- CAREFULLY FRY IN HOT OIL FOR 3-4 MINUTES PER SIDE (WHOLE FISH), UNTIL GOLDEN AND FLOATING.

6. DRAIN AND KEEP WARM

- TRANSFER FRIED FISH TO A WIRE RACK SET OVER PAPER TOWELS.
- KEEP WARM IN A 95°C|200°F OVEN WHILE COOKING NEXT BATCHES.

BIOGRAPHY-BRANDON BERNARD

Last words:

"I WISH I COULD TAKE IT ALL BACK, BUT I CAN'T. I'M SORRY. THAT'S THE ONLY WORDS THAT I CAN SAY THAT COMPLETELY CAPTURE HOW I FEEL NOW AND HOW I FELT THAT DAY."

Brandon Bernard

BORN:	07/03/1980
DIED:	12/10/2020 (AGED 40)
CONVICTIONS:	FIRST-DEGREE MURDER (2 COUNTS). CONSPIRACY TO COMMIT MURDER. CARJACKING RESULTING IN DEATH.
PENALTY:	DEATH

BRANDON ANTHONY MICAH BERNARD (1980-2020) WAS EXECUTED FOR HIS ROLE IN THE 1999 MURDERS OF TODD AND STACIE BAGLEY IN TEXAS. HIS CASE ATTRACTED WIDESPREAD ATTENTION AND APPEALS FOR CLEMENCY DUE TO HIS AGE AT THE TIME OF THE CRIME AND QUESTIONS ABOUT HIS LEVEL OF CULPABILITY.

EARLY LIFE:

- BORN ON JULY 3, 1980, IN TEXAS.
- RAISED IN KILLEEN; DESCRIBED AS QUIET.
- JOINED A GANG AND BECAME INVOLVED IN PETTY CRIMES BEFORE THE MURDER OCCURRED AT AGE 18.

THE CRIME:

- ON JUNE 21, 1999, BERNARD AND SEVERAL ACCOMPLICES ABDUCTED YOUTH MINISTERS TODD AND STACIE BAGLEY IN FORT HOOD, TEXAS.
- THE COUPLE WERE FORCED INTO THE TRUNK OF THEIR CAR.
- ANOTHER ACCOMPLICE SHOT BOTH VICTIMS IN THE HEAD; BERNARD THEN SET THE CAR ON FIRE.
- STACIE BAGLEY MAY HAVE BEEN ALIVE AND UNCONSCIOUS WHEN THE CAR WAS BURNED, LEADING TO BERNARD'S CONVICTION FOR HER MURDER.

ARREST AND TRIAL:

- ARRESTED DAYS AFTER THE MURDERS.
- TRIED IN FEDERAL COURT AND CONVICTED OF CARJACKING RESULTING IN DEATH, AND MURDER.
- IN 2000, HE WAS SENTENCED TO DEATH AT AGE 19, THE YOUNGEST OFFENDER ON FEDERAL DEATH ROW AT THE TIME.

APPEALS AND CONTROVERSY:

- LAWYERS ARGUED BERNARD PLAYED A LESSER ROLE IN THE MURDERS AND THAT HE HAD MATURED REHABILITATED.
- HIS CASE GAINED NATIONAL ATTENTION IN 2020, WITH CLEMENCY PLEAS FROM ACTIVISTS AND LEGAL EXPERTS.
- PRESIDENT TRUMP DECLINED TO INTERVENE.

EXECUTION:

- AT AGE 40, HE WAS ONE OF THE LAST PEOPLE EXECUTED DURING A FEDERAL EXECUTION SPREE IN THE FINAL MONTHS OF THE FIRST TRUMP ADMINISTRATION.

CONVICTED IN 2000.

SPENT 21 YEARS ON DEATH ROW.

EXECUTED BY LETHAL INJECTION ON DECEMBER 10, 2020, AGE 40.

LAST MEAL–BRANDON BERNARD

CRIME: MURDER
STATE: FEDERAL GOVERNMENT
YEAR: 2020
PUNISHMENT: LETHAL INJECTION

REQUESTED LAST MEAL:

MEAT LOVER'S PIZZA AND A BROWNIE.

MEAT LOVER'S PIZZA

INGREDIENTS:

- 120ML|1/2 CUP WATER
- 1/2 TEASPOON ACTIVE DRY YEAST
- 1/4 TEASPOON GRANULATED SUGAR
- 150G|1¼ CUP ALL-PURPOSE FLOUR
- 3/4 TEASPOON SALT
- 1 TABLESPOON OLIVE OIL
- 70–120ML|1/3–1/2 CUP PIZZA SAUCE
- 400G|1½ CUP MOZZARELLA
- 3 TABLESPOON PARMESAN CHEESE
- 3–4 SLICES BACON, COOKED AND CHOPPED
- 75G|1/2 CUP HAM, ROUGHLY CHOPPED
- 75G|1/2 CUP HOT SAUSAGE, COOKED AND CRUMBLED
- 40G|1/4 CUP PEPPERONI SLICES
- GROUND BLACK PEPPER

MEAT LOVER'S PIZZA

1. PREPARE THE DOUGH

- COMBINE WARM WATER 45°C|115°F WITH YEAST AND SUGAR. STIR AND LET PROOF.
- IN A MIXER BOWL, ADD FLOUR AND SALT.
- WITH MIXER ON LOW, SLOWLY ADD YEAST MIXTURE.
- INCREASE SPEED AND ADD OLIVE OIL IF NEEDED. MIX UNTIL DOUGH FORMS A BALL.
- TRANSFER TO A GREASED BOWL, COVER, AND LET RISE IN A WARM PLACE UNTIL DOUBLED (ABOUT 1 HOUR).

2. COOK THE MEATS

- COOK BACON AND SAUSAGE.
- CHOP BACON AND HAM.
- CRUMBLE SAUSAGE.

3. ASSEMBLE THE PIZZA

- PREHEAT OVEN TO 220°C|425°F.
- GREASE A BAKING SHEET WITH OLIVE OIL AND SHAPE DOUGH TO FIT.
- SPREAD PIZZA SAUCE OVER DOUGH.
- SPRINKLE WITH PARMESAN AND 130G|1/2 CUP MOZZARELLA.
- ADD BACON, SAUSAGE, AND HAM.
- TOP WITH REMAINING 100G|1 CUP MOZZARELLA AND A DASH OF BLACK PEPPER.

BIOGRAPHY-SAMUEL FLIPPEN

NO LAST WORDS.
LOCKED EYES WITH HIS PARENTS, SMILED, AND MOUTHED "I LOVE YOU" THREE TIMES BEFORE CLOSING HIS EYES.

Samuel Flippen

BORN:	09/30/1969
DIED:	08/18/2006 (AGED 36)
CONVICTIONS:	FIRST-DEGREE MURDER
PENALTY:	DEATH

SAMUEL RUSSELL FLIPPEN (1969-2006) WAS AN AMERICAN MAN EXECUTED BY NORTH CAROLINA FOR THE 1994 KILLING OF HIS TWO-YEAR-OLD STEPDAUGHTER. HIS CASE REMAINS HIGHLY CONTROVERSIAL, RAISING QUESTIONS ABOUT EVIDENCE RELIABILITY AND THE FAIRNESS OF HIS CONVICTION.

EARLY LIFE:

- BORN SEPTEMBER 30, 1969, IN FORSYTH COUNTY, NORTH CAROLINA.
- WORKED VARIOUS JOBS; HAD NO PRIOR CRIMINAL RECORD BEFORE THE INCIDENT.

THE CRIME:

- ON FEBRUARY 12, 1994, HIS WIFE LEFT HIM ALONE WITH HIS STEP-DAUGHTER, BRITNIE NICHOLE HUTTON.
- FLIPPEN LATER CALLED 911, CLAIMING SHE HAD FALLEN.
- MEDICAL EXAMINERS DETERMINED BRITNIE SUFFERED FATAL BLUNT-FORCE INJURIES INCONSISTENT WITH A FALL.

ARREST AND TRIAL:

- CHARGED WITH FIRST-DEGREE MURDER; DECLINED A PLEA TO A LESSER CHARGE.
- MEDICAL TECHNICIANS TESTIFIED THAT INJURIES WERE INFLICTED UP TO 12 HOURS BEFORE DEATH.
- A RETRIAL WAS LATER ORDERED TO CONSIDER HIS CLEAN RECORD, BUT A SECOND JURY SENTENCED HIM TO DEATH.

EXECUTION:

- MAINTAINED HIS INNOCENCE TO THE END AND HAD NO OFFICIAL FINAL STATEMENT.

LEGACY:

- BRITNIE'S BIOLOGICAL FATHER LATER RAISED CONCERNS ABOUT OVERLOOKED EVIDENCE AND POSSIBLE ABUSE BY THE VICTIM'S MOTHER, AS ANOTHER WITNESS HAD TESTIFIED THAT HER OTHER CHILD SHOWED SIGNS OF PHYSICAL ABUSE, YEARS AFTER FLIPPEN WAS EXECUTED.
- THE CASE IS FREQUENTLY CITED IN DEBATES OVER DEATH PENALTY FAIRNESS, AND WRONGFUL CONVICTION.

CONVICTED OF MURDER, 1995.

SPENT 11 YEARS ON DEATH ROW.

EXECUTED BY LETHAL INJECTION ON AUGUST 18, 2006, AT AGE 36.

LAST MEAL -SAMUEL FLIPPEN

CRIME: MURDER
STATE: NORTH CAROLINA
YEAR: 2006
PUNISHMENT: LETHAL INJECTION

REQUESTED LAST MEAL:

POPCORN SHRIMP, HUSH PUPPIES, FRENCH FRIES, AND A COKE.

POPCORN SHRIMP

INGREDIENTS:

- 450G|1 LB SMALL SHRIMP, PELLED AND DEVEINED
- 190G|1¼ CUPS ALL-PURPOSE FLOUR
- 2 TEASPOONS SALT PLUS MORE FOR SERVING
- 1/2 TEASPOON PAPRIKA, SMOKED OR REGULAR
- 1/4 TEASPOON PEPPER
- 1/4 TEASPOON GARLIC POWDER
- 1 EGG
- 60ML|1/4 CUP MILK
- VEGETABLE OIL FOR FRYING
- 2 TEASPOONS FRESH PARSLEY, CHOPPED

POPCORN SHRIMP

1. MIX SEASONED FLOUR
   - IN A MEDIUM BOWL, COMBINE FLOUR, SALT, PAPRIKA, PEPPER, AND GARLIC POWDER.

2. COAT SHRIMP
   - PAT SHRIMP DRY.
   - TOSS WITH 30G|1/4 CUP OF THE FLOUR MIXTURE TO LIGHTLY COAT.

3. HEAT OIL
   - HEAT 8-10CM|3-4 INCHES OF OIL IN A DEEP POT TO 190°C|375°F.

4. BREAD SHRIMP
   - WHISK TOGETHER EGG AND MILK.
   - DIP SHRIMP INTO MILK MIXTURE, THEN DREDGE IN REMAINING FLOUR MIXTURE.

5. FRY & SERVE
   - FRY SHRIMP IN BATCHES FOR 2-3 MINUTES UNTIL GOLDEN BROWN.
   - DRAIN ON PAPER TOWELS.
   - SPRINKLE WITH PARSLEY AND SERVE HOT.

BIOGRAPHY-RICKY RAY RECTOR

RICKY RAY RECTOR (1950-1992) WAS EXECUTED IN ARKANSAS FOR THE 1981 KILLING OF A MAN AND A POLICE OFFICER. HIS EXECUTION DREW NATIONAL CONTROVERSY DUE TO HIS SEVERE MENTAL IMPAIRMENT FOLLOWING A SUICIDE ATTEMPT, AND IT REMAINS ONE OF THE MOST DEBATED CAPITAL PUNISHMENT CASES IN U.S. HISTORY.

BORN:	01/12/1950
DIED:	01/24/1992 (AGED 42)
CONVICTIONS:	CAPITAL MURDER
PENALTY:	DEATH

EARLY LIFE:

- BORN JANUARY 12, 1950, IN CONWAY, ARKANSAS.
- GREW UP IN A WORKING-CLASS FAMILY; DESCRIBED AS SHY, QUIET, AND INTELLECTUALLY LIMITED.
- STRUGGLED IN SCHOOL AND WAS EXPELLED IN THE TENTH GRADE.
- REPORTEDLY ENDURED PHYSICAL ABUSE DURING CHILDHOOD.

THE CRIME:

- ON MARCH 21, 1981, RECTOR GOT INTO AN ARGUMENT AT A LOCAL RESTAURANT AND FATALLY SHOT A MAN NAMED ARTHUR CRISWELL.
- FLED AND HID FOR THREE DAYS BEFORE AGREEING TO SURRENDER TO POLICE.
- ON MARCH 24, DURING THE ATTEMPTED ARREST, HE SHOT AND KILLED POLICE OFFICER ROBERT MARTIN, THEN TURNED THE GUN ON HIMSELF IN A SUICIDE ATTEMPT.
- THE BULLET DESTROYED PART OF HIS BRAIN'S FRONTAL LOBE, LEAVING HIM PERMANENTLY COGNITIVELY IMPAIRED.

ARREST AND TRIAL:

- DESPITE SEVERE BRAIN DAMAGE, RECTOR SURVIVED.
- CONVICTED OF BOTH MURDERS: SENTENCED TO LIFE IMPRISONMENT FOR THE FIRST AND DEATH FOR THE SECOND.
- DISPLAYED SIGNIFICANT SIGNS OF MENTAL DISABILITY, INCLUDING MEMORY LOSS, DISORIENTATION, AND CHILDLIKE BEHAVIOR.

EXECUTION:

- FOR HIS LAST MEAL, HE LEFT THE PIE UNTOUCHED, SAYING HE WAS "SAVING IT FOR LATER."
- PRISON OFFICIALS STRUGGLED FOR OVER 50 MINUTES TO FIND A USABLE VEIN, INCREASING THE PHYSICAL AND EMOTIONAL DISTRESS OF THE PROCESS.

CONVICTED OF MURDER, 1982.

SPENT 9 YEARS ON DEATH ROW.

EXECUTED BY LETHAL INJECTION ON JANUARY 24, 1992, IN ARKANSAS.

CRIME: MURDER
STATE: ARKANSAS
YEAR: 1992
PUNISHMENT: LETHAL INJECTION

REQUESTED LAST MEAL:

STEAK, FRIED CHICKEN, CHERRY KOOL-AID, AND A PECAN PIE. HE DID NOT EAT THE PIE BECAUSE HE WAS 'SAVING IT FOR LATER'.

PECAN PIE

INGREDIENTS:

- 1 UNBAKED FLAKY PIE CRUST
- EGG WASH FOR PIE CRUST:1 LARGE EGG BEATEN WITH 1 TABLESPOON MILK OR HEAVY CREAM
- 250G|2½ CUPS SHELLED PECANS
- 3 LARGE EGGS
- 240ML|1 CUP DARK CORN SYRUP
- 100G|1/2 CUP LIGHT OR DARK BROWN SUGAR
- 1½ TEASPOONS PURE VANILLA EXTRACT
- 55G|1/4 CUP UNSALTED BUTTER, MELTED AND SLIGHTLY COOLED
- 1/2 TEASPOON SALT
- 1/2 TEASPOON GROUND CINNAMON

PECAN PIE

1. PREPARE THE CRUST

- ROLL OUT CHILLED PIE DOUGH INTO A 30CM|12-INCH CIRCLE.
- TRANSFER TO A 23CM|9-INCH PIE DISH, TUCK AND CRIMP EDGES AS DESIRED.
- BRUSH EDGES WITH EGG WASH.
- CHILL IN THE DISH FOR 10 MINUTES.
- PREHEAT OVEN TO 177°C|350°F, RACK IN LOWER THIRD.

2. MAKE THE FILLING

- CHOP PECANS ROUGHLY AND SPREAD EVENLY INSIDE THE PREPARED PIE CRUST.
- IN A BOWL, WHISK TOGETHER EGGS, CORN SYRUP, BROWN SUGAR, VANILLA, MELTED BUTTER, SALT, AND CINNAMON UNTIL WELL COMBINED.
- POUR THE MIXTURE OVER THE PECANS.

3. BAKE AND COOL

- BAKE FOR 50-55 MINUTES UNTIL TOP IS LIGHTLY BROWNED.
- AFTER 20 MINUTES, COVER EDGES WITH A PIE SHIELD OR FOIL TO PREVENT OVER-BROWNING.
- COOL COMPLETELY ON A WIRE RACK.

3. SERVE AND STORE

- SLICE AND SERVE WARM OR ROOM TEMP WITH WHIPPED CREAM OR ICE CREAM. ENJOY.

LAST MEAL–ROBERT DALE CONKLIN

CRIME: MALICE MURDER
STATE: GEORGIA
YEAR: 2008
PUNISHMENT: LETHAL INJECTION

REQUESTED LAST MEAL:

FILET MIGNON STEAK WRAPPED IN BACON, DE-VEINED SHRIMP SAUTEED IN GARLIC BUTTER WITH LEMON; A BAKED POTATO FILLED WITH SOUR CREAM, CHIVES AND BACON BITS; CORN ON THE COB; ASPARAGUS WITH HOLLANDAISE SAUCE; A BUTTERED FRENCH BAGUETTE WITH GOAT'S CHEESE; CANTALOUPE; APPLE PIE; VANILLA BEAN ICE CREAM, AND ICED TEA.

FILET MIGNON WRAPPED IN BACON

INGREDIENTS:

- 4 (4CM|1½-INCH THICK) FILET MIGNON STEAKS
- 4 STRIPS THIN-CUT BACON
- 4 SMALL TOOTHPICKS
- 1/2 TEASPOON SALT

METHOD

FILET MIGNON WRAPPED IN BACON

1. WRAP & SEASON

- WRAP EACH FILET WITH 1 STRIP OF BACON, SECURE WITH A TOOTHPICK.
- TRIM ANY EXCESS BACON AND SAVE IT FOR COOKING.
- SEASON FILETS WITH SALT (AVOID SALTING BACON).
- REFRIGERATE OR COOK IMMEDIATELY.

2. RENDER BACON FAT

- PREHEAT CAST IRON SKILLET OVER MEDIUM HEAT.
- COOK RESERVED BACON UNTIL FAT RENDERS AND PAN IS COATED.
- REMOVE AND DISCARD BACON.

3. SEAL BACON

- REMOVE TOOTHPICKS FROM FILETS.
- PLACE FILETS ON BACON OVERLAP EDGE IN PAN.
- COOK 30 SECONDS UNTIL BACON CRISPS AND SEALS.
- TURN FILETS EVERY 30 SECONDS TO CRISP BACON EVENLY.

4. COOK FILETS

- STAND FILETS UPRIGHT.
- COOK 4-8 MINUTES PER SIDE (4=RARE, 6=MEDIUM, 8=WELL DONE).

5. FINAL SEAR & REST

- SEAR BACON SIDES QUICKLY TO CRISP ALL AROUND.
- TRANSFER TO CUTTING BOARD AND REST FOR 6 MINUTES.
- SERVE HOT.

LAST MEAL–SEAN RICHARD SELLERS

CRIME:	SERIAL MURDER
STATE:	OKLAHOMA
YEAR:	1999
PUNISHMENT:	LETHAL INJECTION

REQUESTED LAST MEAL:

EGGROLLS, SWEET AND SOUR SHRIMP, AND BATTER-FRIED SHRIMP.

EGG ROLLS

INGREDIENTS:

- 2 TEASPOONS VEGETABLE OIL
- 340G|3/4 LB GROUND PORK
- SALT AND PEPPER TO TASTE
- 1 TEASPOON GARLIC, MINCED
- 630G|3 CUPS COLESLAW MIX
- 26G|1/4 CUP GREEN ONIONS, SLICED
- 1 TABLESPOON SOY SAUCE
- 1 TEASPOON TOASTED SESAME OIL
- 12 EGG ROLL WRAPPERS
- 1 EGG, BEATEN
- OIL FOR FRYING

EGG ROLLS

1. COOK THE FILLING

- HEAT VEGETABLE OIL IN A LARGE PAN OVER MEDIUM-HIGH HEAT.
- ADD GROUND PORK, SEASON WITH SALT AND PEPPER, AND COOK UNTIL BROWNED.
- ADD GARLIC AND GINGER; COOK FOR 30 SECONDS.
- STIR IN COLESLAW MIX AND GREEN ONIONS. COOK UNTIL CABBAGE IS WILTED, ABOUT 3-4 MINUTES.
- ADD SOY SAUCE AND SESAME OIL, THEN REMOVE FROM HEAT.

2. FILL AND WRAP

- SPOON 2-3 TABLESPOONS OF FILLING ONTO EACH EGG ROLL WRAPPER.
- FOLD ACCORDING TO PACKAGE DIRECTIONS, SEALING EDGES WITH BEATEN EGG.

3. FRY AND SERVE

- HEAT 2-3 INCHES OF OIL IN A DEEP POT TO 175°C|350°F.
- FRY EGG ROLLS IN BATCHES, TURNING OCCASIONALLY, UNTIL GOLDEN BROWN (ABOUT 3-5 MINUTES).
- DRAIN ON PAPER TOWELS AND SERVE WITH YOUR FAVORITE DIPPING SAUCE.

BIOGRAPHY-DOBIE GILLIS WILLIAMS

Last words:
"I JUST WANT TO SAY, I DON'T HAVE ANY HARD FEELINGS AGAINST ANYBODY. GOD BLESS Y'ALL. GOD BLESS."

Dobie Gillis Williams

BORN:	1961
DIED:	01/08/1999 (AGED 37-38)
CONVICTIONS:	FIRST-DEGREE MURDER
PENALTY:	DEATH

DOBIE GILLIS WILLIAMS (1961-1999) WAS EXECUTED IN LOUISIANA FOR THE 1984 MURDER OF SONJA KNIPPERS. HIS CASE WAS CONTROVERSIAL DUE TO QUESTIONS RAISED ABOUT HIS INTELLECTUAL CAPACITY, POSSIBLE POLICE MISCONDUCT, AND THE FAIRNESS OF HIS TRIAL.

EARLY LIFE:

- BORN IN 1961 AND GREW UP IN LOUISIANA.
- HAD AN INTELLECTUAL DISABILITY, WITH LOW IQ.
- SERVED TIME FOR BURGLARY AND WAS OUT ON A FIVE-DAY PRISON FURLOUGH AT THE TIME OF THE CRIME.

THE CRIME:

- ON JULY 8, 1984, AN INTRUDER ENTERED THE KNIPPERS FAMILY HOME THROUGH A BATHROOM WINDOW, RAPED AND FATALLY STABBED SONJA KNIPPERS.
- WITNESSES LATER SAID THE ATTACKER WAS A BLACK MAN.

ARREST AND TRAIL:

- WILLIAMS WAS STAYING NEARBY WHEN POLICE PICKED HIM UP FOR QUESTIONING.
- OFFICERS CLAIMED HE CONFESSED DURING UNRECORDED INTERROGATIONS, LEADING THEM TO FIND THE MURDER WEAPON AND HIS SHIRT.
- FORENSIC EVIDENCE INCLUDED BLOOD ON A BATHROOM CURTAIN MATCHING HIS RARE BLOOD TYPE AND HAIR MATCHING WILLIAMS.
- TRIED BY AN ALL-WHITE JURY, HE WAS CONVICTED OF FIRST-DEGREE MURDER AND SENTENCED TO DEATH.

APPEALS:

- A FEDERAL JUDGE OVERTURNED HIS SENTENCE, BUT THE 5TH CIRCUIT REINSTATED IT UNDER AEDPA RULES, CITING LATE SUBMISSION OF MITIGATING EVIDENCE.

CONVICTED OF MURDER, 1985.

SPENT 14 YEARS ON DEATH ROW.

EXECUTED BY LETHAL INJECTION ON JANUARY 8, 1999, IN LOUISIANA.

LAST MEAL-DOBIE GILLIS WILLIAMS

CRIME: MURDER
STATE: LOUISIANA
YEAR: 1999
PUNISHMENT: LETHAL INJECTION

REQUESTED LAST MEAL:

TWELVE CHOCOLATE BARS AND SOME ICE CREAM.

HOMEMADE ICE CREAM

INGREDIENTS:

- 284ML|10 OZ CARTON DOUBLE CREAM
- 300ML|10.5 OZ FULL FAT MILK
- 115G|4 OZ GOLDEN SUGAR
- 1 VANILLA POD
- 3 LARGE FREE-RANGE EGG YOLKS
- LOTS OF ICE CUBES

METHOD

HOMEMADE ICE CREAM

1. HEAT CREAM

- IN A PAN, COMBINE CREAM, MILK, HALF THE SUGAR, VANILLA SEEDS, AND POD.
- HEAT ON LOW UNTIL ALMOST BOILING. REMOVE FROM HEAT AND LET INFUSE FOR 30 MINUTES.

2. MAKE EGG MIXTURE

- BEAT EGG YOLKS WITH REMAINING SUGAR FOR 2 MINUTES UNTIL PALE AND THICK.
- ADD A SMALL AMOUNT OF THE WARM CREAM MIXTURE TO THE EGGS AND MIX.
- THEN STIR THE EGG MIXTURE BACK INTO THE PAN.

3. COOK CUSTARD

- RETURN TO LOW HEAT. STIR CONSTANTLY FOR 8-10 MINUTES UNTIL CUSTARD THICKENS.
- DO NOT LET IT BOIL. REMOVE FROM HEAT ONCE IT COATS THE BACK OF A SPOON.

4. COOL & CHILL

- POUR CUSTARD INTO A BOWL. PLACE OVER ICE WATER TO COOL FOR 20 MINUTES, STIRRING OCCASIONALLY.
- REFRIGERATE FOR 3-4 HOURS OR OVERNIGHT UNTIL VERY COLD.

5. WHIP AND FREEZE

- WHIP CREAM UNTIL LIGHT. FOLD INTO COLD CUSTARD. FREEZE 3-4 HOURS, STIRRING HOURLY UNTIL NEARLY FIRM.

BIOGRAPHY-RONALD CLARK O'BRYAN

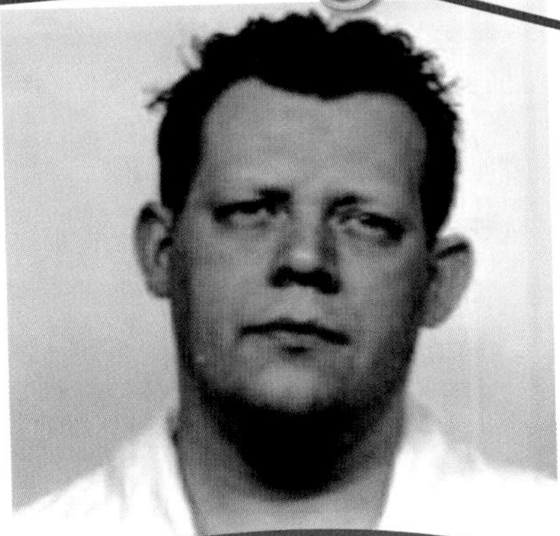

Ronald Clark O'Bryan

"WHAT IS ABOUT TO TRANSPIRE IN A FEW MOMENTS IS WRONG! HOWEVER, WE AS HUMAN BEINGS DO MAKE MISTAKES AND ERRORS. THIS EXECUTION IS ONE OF THOSE WRONGS YET DOESN'T MEAN OUR WHOLE SYSTEM OF JUSTICE IS WRONG. THEREFORE, I WOULD FORGIVE ALL WHO HAVE TAKEN PART IN ANY WAY IN MY DEATH.

ALSO, TO ANYONE I HAVE OFFENDED IN ANY WAY DURING MY 39 YEARS, I PRAY AND ASK YOUR FORGIVENESS, JUST AS I FORGIVE ANYONE WHO OFFENDED ME IN ANY WAY. AND I PRAY AND ASK GOD'S FORGIVENESS FOR ALL OF US RESPECTIVELY AS HUMAN BEINGS.

TO MY LOVED ONES, I EXTEND MY UNDYING LOVE. TO THOSE CLOSE TO ME, KNOW IN YOUR HEARTS I LOVE YOU ONE AND ALL. GOD BLESS YOU ALL AND MAY GOD'S BEST BLESSINGS BE ALWAYS YOURS. RONALD C. O'BRYAN P.S. DURING MY TIME HERE, I HAVE BEEN TREATED WELL BY ALL T.D.C. PERSONNEL."

Last words

AKA:	THE CANDY MAN, THE MAN WHO KILLED HALLOWEEN, THE PIXY STIX KILLER
BORN:	10/19/1944
DIED:	03/31/1984 (AGED 39)
CONVICTIONS:	CAPITAL MURDER. ATTEMPTED MURDER (4 COUNTS)
PENALTY:	DEATH

RONALD CLARK O'BRYAN (1944-1984) WAS A CONVICTED MURDERER EXECUTED FOR KILLING HIS 8-YEAR-OLD SON WITH POISONED HALLOWEEN CANDY IN 1974. DUBBED "THE CANDY MAN" OR "THE MAN WHO KILLED HALLOWEEN".

EARLY LIFE:

- BORN ON OCTOBER 19, 1944, IN TEXAS.
- WORKED AS AN OPTICIAN AND WAS ACTIVE IN HIS LOCAL CHURCH.
- MARRIED WITH TWO CHILDREN, WAS STRUGGLING FINANCIALLY AND DEEPLY IN DEBT.
- A FEW DAYS BEFORE HIS SON'S DEATH, HE HAD ACCRUED MULTIPLE INSURANCE POLICIES ON HIS CHILDREN TOTALING OVER $60,000.

THE CRIME:

- ON OCTOBER 31, 1974, O'BRYAN GAVE HIS CHILDREN AND THREE OTHER KIDS PIXY STIX LACED WITH POTASSIUM CYANIDE WHILE TRICK-OR-TREATING IN PASADENA, TEXAS.
- HIS 8-YEAR-OLD SON, TIMOTHY, CONSUMED THE POISONED CANDY AND DIED WITHIN AN HOUR.

ARREST AND TRIAL:

- ARRESTED DAYS AFTER HIS SON'S FUNERAL AND CHARGED WITH MURDER AND ATTEMPTED MURDER.
- EVIDENCE SHOWED HE HAD PURCHASED CYANIDE AND RESEARCHED POISONS.

CONVICTED OF MURDER, 1975.

SPENT 8 YEARS ON DEATH ROW.

EXECUTED BY LETHAL INJECTION ON MARCH 31, 1984, IN TEXAS.

LAST MEAL–RONALD CLARK O'BRYAN

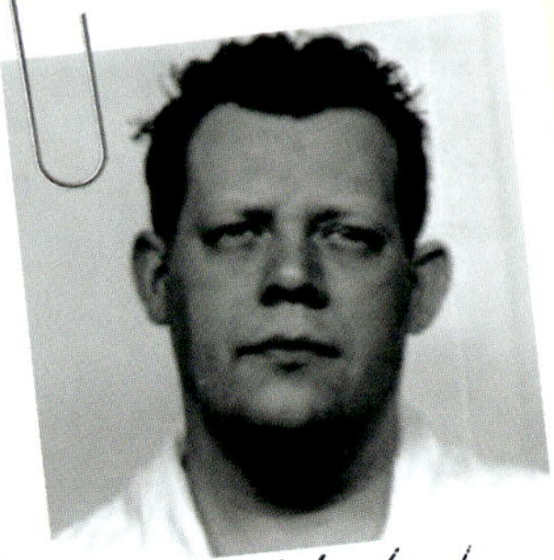

Ronald Clark O'Bryan

AKA: THE CANDY MA
CRIME: MURDE
STATE: TEXA
YEAR: 198
PUNISHMENT: LETHAL INJECTIO

REQUESTED LAST MEAL

T-BONE STEAK (MEDIUM TO WELL DONE), FRENCH FRIES AND KETCHUP, WHOLE KERNEL CORN, SWEET PEAS, LETTUCE AND TOMATO SALAD WITH EGG AND FRENCH DRESSING, ICED TEA, SWEETENER, SALTINES, BOSTON CREAM PIE, AND ROLLS

T-BONE STEAK

INGREDIENTS:

- 2 WHOLE T-BONE STEAKS, AT LEAST 4CM|1½ IN THICK
- KOSHER SALT AND FRESHLY GROUND BLACK PEPPER

LAST MEAL

O'BRYAN'S CASE BECAME A LASTING PART OF AMERICAN FOLKLORE AND IS OFTEN CITED IN WARNINGS ABOUT HALLOWEEN CANDY SAFETY.

T-BONE STEAK

METHOD

1. SEASON THE STEAKS

- SEASON STEAKS GENEROUSLY WITH SALT AND PEPPER ON ALL SIDES.
- PLACE ON A WIRE RACK OVER A BAKING SHEET AND REFRIGERATE UNCOVERED FOR AT LEAST 45 MINUTES (OR SEASON JUST BEFORE GRILLING).

2. PREPARE THE GRILL

- LIGHT A CHIMNEY OF CHARCOAL AND POUR HOT COALS ON ONE SIDE OF THE GRILL.
- (ALTERNATIVELY, SET HALF OF GAS GRILL BURNERS TO HIGH.)
- PLACE COOKING GRATE, COVER, AND PREHEAT FOR 5 MINUTES.
- CLEAN AND OIL THE GRATE.

3. COOK ON INDIRECT HEAT

- PLACE STEAKS ON COOLER SIDE OF GRILL WITH TENDERLOIN SIDE FARTHEST FROM COALS.
- COVER GRILL WITH VENTS HALF-CLOSED.
- COOK, TURNING ONCE, UNTIL STRIP SIDE REGISTERS 46°C|115°F AND TENDERLOIN 43°C|110°F, ABOUT 15 MINUTES.(START CHECKING AFTER 10 MINUTES.)

4. SEAR OVER HIGH HEAT

- IF NEEDED, ADD MORE COALS TO REIGNITE HIGH HEAT.
- MOVE STEAKS DIRECTLY OVER COALS AND SEAR BOTH SIDES WELL.
- USE TONGS TO SEAR EDGES TOO.

5. REST AND SERVE

- TRANSFER STEAKS TO A CUTTING BOARD.
- LET REST FOR 10 MINUTES.
- SLICE AND SERVE HOT.

BIOGRAPHY-PHILIP RAY WORKMAN

"I'VE PRAYED TO THE LORD JESUS CHRIST NOT TO LAY CHARGE OF MY DEATH TO ANY MAN."

2 MINUTES AFTER THE START OF THE INJECTIONS:
"I COMMEND MY SPIRIT INTO YOUR HANDS, LORD JESUS CHRIST."

Philip Ray Workman

Last words

BORN:	06/01/1953
DIED:	05/09/2007 (AGED 53)
CONVICTIONS:	FIRST-DEGREE MURDER. AGGRAVATED ASSAULT. BURGLARY
PENALTY:	DEATH

PHILIP RAY WORKMAN (1953-2007) WAS EXECUTED IN TENNESSEE FOR THE 1981 MURDER OF A POLICE OFFICER DURING A BOTCHED ROBBERY. HIS CASE ATTRACTED WIDESPREAD ATTENTION AND CONTROVERSY DUE TO CONFLICTING EVIDENCE, QUESTIONS ABOUT POLICE CONDUCT, AND CLAIMS OF HIS INNOCENCE. IT BECAME A PROMINENT EXAMPLE IN THE DEBATE OVER CAPITAL PUNISHMENT AND WRONGFUL CONVICTIONS.

EARLY LIFE:

- BORN JUNE 1, 1953, IN TENNESSEE.
- SERVED IN THE U.S. ARMY AND DEVELOPED A DRUG ADDICTION DURING HIS SERVICE.
- AFTER LEAVING THE MILITARY, STRUGGLED WITH SUBSTANCE ABUSE, UNEMPLOYMENT, HOMELESSNESS, AND PETTY CRIME.

THE CRIME:

- ON AUGUST 5, 1981, WORKMAN ATTEMPTED TO ROB A WENDY'S RESTAURANT IN MEMPHIS, TENNESSEE, ARMED WITH A SEMI-AUTOMATIC PISTOL.
- DURING HIS ESCAPE, POLICE OFFICERS RESPONDED TO THE SCENE AND CONFRONTED HIM IN THE PARKING LOT.
- IN THE EXCHANGE, LIEUTENANT RONALD OLIVER WAS FATALLY SHOT.

ARREST AND TRIAL:

- CHARGED WITH AND CONVICTED OF THE FIRST-DEGREE MURDER OF LT. OLIVER IN 1982.
- A KEY MEDICAL EXAMINER LATER RECANTED HIS TESTIMONY, STATING THAT EVIDENCE SUGGESTED THE FATAL BULLET DIDN'T COME FROM WORKMAN'S GUN, AND FRIENDLY FIRE MIGHT HAVE KILLED OLIVER.
- A KEY WITNESS WHO 'SAW' WORKMAN SHOOT OLIVER WAS NOT SEEN ON THE SCENE BY ANYBODY THERE.

CONVICTED OF MURDER, 1982.

SPENT 25 YEARS ON DEATH ROW.

EXECUTED BY LETHAL INJECTION ON MAY 09, 2007, IN TENNESSEE.

LAST MEAL–PHILIP RAY WORKMAN

CRIME: FIRST DEGREE MURDER
STATE: TENNESSEE
YEAR: 2007
PUNISHMENT: LETHAL INJECTION

REQUESTED LAST MEAL:

VEGETARIAN PIZZA

VEGETARIAN PIZZA

INGREDIENTS:

- 400–450G|14–16 OZ BALL PIZZA DOUGH
- 120ML|1/2 CUP MARINARA SAUCE
- 1 TABLESPOON FRESH BASIL, FINELY CHOPPED
- 1 TABLESPOON OREGANO
- 115G| 1 CUP SHREDDED MOZZARELLA CHEESE
- 1/4 MEDIUM RED ONION, THINLY SLICED
- 35G|1/4 CUP SLICED BLACK OLIVES
- 1/2 MEDIUM TOMATO, CHOPPED
- KOSHER SALT
- FRESHLY GROUND BLACK PEPPER

VEGETARIAN PIZZA

1. PREHEAT THE OVEN

- PREHEAT OVEN TO 260°C|500°F IF USING A BAKING SHEET, OR AS HIGH AS IT WILL GO IF USING A BAKING STONE OR STEEL.
- PLACE STONE OR STEEL IN THE BOTTOM THIRD OF THE OVEN.
- LET OVEN PREHEAT FOR AT LEAST 30 MINUTES.
- IF USING STONE OR STEEL, SWITCH TO LET OVEN PREHEAT FOR AT LEAST 30 MINUTES. IF USING STONE OR STEEL, SWITCH TO BROIL ON HIGH JUST BEFORE BAKING.

2. PREPARE THE DOUGH

- STRETCH OR ROLL DOUGH INTO A 30-35CM|12-14 INCH CIRCLE.
- TRANSFER TO A BAKING SHEET OR LIGHTLY FLOURED PIZZA PEEL.

3. ADD TOPPINGS

- SPREAD SAUCE OVER DOUGH, LEAVING A 1CM|1/2 INCH BORDER.
- ADD CHOPPED FRESH HERBS AND HALF THE CHEESE.
- LAYER ONION, MUSHROOMS, BELL PEPPER, OLIVES, REMAINING CHEESE, AND TOMATO.
- SEASON WITH SALT AND BLACK PEPPER.

4. BAKE

- TRANSFER PIZZA TO OVEN.
- BAKE 8-10 MINUTES ON BAKING SHEET OR 6-8 MINUTES ON STONE/STEEL, UNTIL CRUST IS GOLDEN AND BOTTOM IS BROWNED.

5. SERVE

- REMOVE FROM OVEN AND LET REST A COUPLE MINUTES.
- SLICE AND SERVE.

CRIME: MURDER
STATE: NEBRASKA
YEAR: 2018
PUNISHMENT: LETHAL INJECTION

REQUESTED LAST MEAL:

PIZZA WITH BACON, BEEF, CHEESE, AND MUSHROOMS, PEPSI, AND STRAWBERRY CHEESECAKE.

STRAWBERRY CHEESECAKE INGREDIENTS:

- 250G|8.8 OZ GRAHAM CRACKERS
- 100G|3.5 OZ BUTTER, MELTED
- 1 VANILLA POD
- 600G|1.3LBS FULL-FAT SOFT CHEESE
- 100G|3.5 OZ CONFECTIONERS' SUGAR
- 284ML|10 OZ POT DOUBLE CREAM
- 400G|14 OZ STRAWBERRIES, HALVED
- 25G|0.8 OZ CONFECTIONERS' SUGAR

STRAWBERRY CHEESECAKE

1. MAKE THE BASE

- CRUSH GRAHAM CRACKERS INTO CRUMBS AND MIX WITH MELTED BUTTER.
- PRESS INTO A BUTTERED, LINED 23CM|9 INCH SPRINGFORM TIN.
- CHILL FOR 1 HOUR UNTIL FIRMED UP.

2. PREP THE FILLING

- SCRAPE VANILLA SEEDS FROM POD.
- WHISK DOUBLE CREAM TO SOFT PEAKS.
- IN A SEPARATE BOWL, BEAT SOFT CHEESE, CONFECTIONERS' SUGAR, AND VANILLA SEEDS UNTIL SMOOTH.
- FOLD IN WHIPPED CREAM UNTIL THICK.
- SPOON OVER BASE AND SMOOTH THE TOP.
- CHILL OVERNIGHT TO SET.

3. FINISH & SERVE

- BRING TO ROOM TEMP FOR 30 MINUTES.
- REMOVE FROM TIN AND TRANSFER TO A PLATE.
- BLEND HALF THE STRAWBERRIES WITH CONFECTIONERS' SUGAR AND A SPLASH OF WATER TO MAKE A PURÉE.
- TOP CHEESECAKE WITH REMAINING STRAWBERRIES AND DRIZZLE WITH PURÉE.

LAST MEAL–BRIAN DAVID STECKEL

CRIME: MURDER
STATE: DELAWARE
YEAR: 2005
PUNISHMENT: LETHAL INJECTION

REQUESTED LAST MEAL:

CHEESESTEAK, COLESLAW, AND A PEPSI-COLA.

PHILLY CHEESESTEAK

INGREDIENTS:

- 455G|1 LB BONELESS RIB EYE OR SKIRT STEAK
- 1 TABLESPOON VEGETABLE OIL
- 1/2 MEDIUM YELLOW ONION, DICED
- 8 THIN SLICES PROVOLONE CHEESE, 4 SLICES TORN INTO 2.5CM|1-INCH SLICES, 4 SLICES WHOLE
- 2 TABLESPOONS PARMESAN
- 1 TEASPOON KOSHER SALT
- 1/8 TEASPOON FRESHLY GROUND BLACK PEPPER
- 2 ITALIAN SUB ROLLS, SLICED ON ONE SIDE

PHILLY CHEESESTEAK

1. PREP THE STEAK

- IF USING A WHOLE STEAK, TRIM AND SLICE INTO 8CM|3-INCH WIDE SECTIONS. FREEZE UNTIL FIRM, ABOUT 1 HOUR.
- IF USING PRE-SLICED STEAK, SKIP TO NEXT STEP.

2. SLICE & CHOP

- SHAVE STEAK THINLY AGAINST THE GRAIN.
- PILE MEAT ON THE CUTTING BOARD AND CHOP COARSELY:
- ABOUT 5 TIMES FOR STORE-BOUGHT SLICES, 10 TIMES FOR HAND-SLICED.

3. COOK MEAT & ONIONS

- HEAT A CAST-IRON SKILLET OVER MEDIUM-HIGH FOR 5 MINUTES.
- ADD OIL, THEN MEAT AND ONION IN AN EVEN LAYER.
- COOK WITHOUT STIRRING FOR 4-6 MINUTES UNTIL WELL BROWNED ON ONE SIDE.
- STIR FREQUENTLY UNTIL MEAT IS NO LONGER PINK AND ONIONS ARE BROWNED, 2-4 MINUTES.

4. ADD CHEESE & SEASONINGS

- STIR IN TORN PROVOLONE, PARMESAN (IF USING), SALT, AND PEPPER.
- COOK, STIRRING CONSTANTLY, UNTIL MELTED AND WELL COMBINED, 1-2 MINUTES.
- DIVIDE INTO 2 PORTIONS SHAPED TO MATCH ROLL LENGTH.
- PLACE 2 SLICES OF PROVOLONE OVER EACH PORTION. COVER TO MELT, ABOUT 1 MINUTE.

5. ASSEMBLE & SERVE

- PLACE ROLLS CUT SIDE DOWN OVER EACH PORTION.
- USE A SPATULA TO SCOOP AND FLIP THE MEAT INTO THE ROLL.
- SERVE IMMEDIATELY.

STANLEY TOOKIE WILLIAMS III (1953-2005) WAS A CO-FOUNDER OF THE CRIPS GANG IN LOS ANGELES WHO WAS CONVICTED OF FOUR MURDERS DURING A 1979 ROBBERY SPREE. AFTER DECADES ON DEATH ROW, HE BECAME AN ANTI-GANG ACTIVIST, AUTHOR, AND NOBEL PEACE PRIZE NOMINEE BEFORE BEING EXECUTED IN CALIFORNIA.

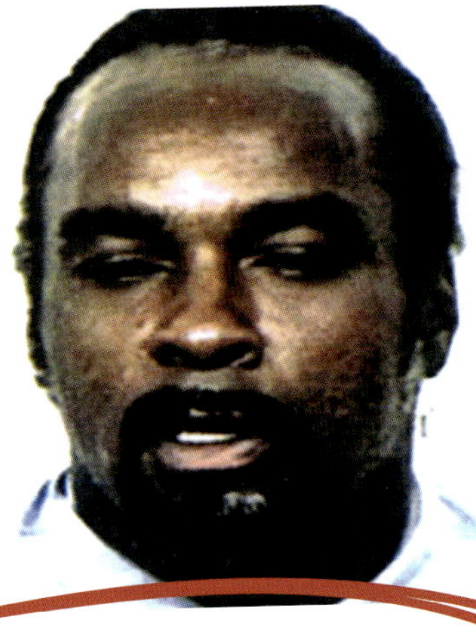

Stanley Tookie Williams

BORN:	12/29/1953
DIED:	12/13/2005 (AGED 51)
CONVICTIONS:	FIRST-DEGREE MURDER WITH SPECIAL CIRCUMSTANCES (4 COUNTS)
PENALTY:	DEATH

EARLY LIFE:

- BORN DECEMBER 29, 1953, IN NEW ORLEANS; RAISED IN SOUTH CENTRAL LOS ANGELES.
- GREW UP LARGELY UNSUPERVISED, BECOMING INVOLVED IN GANG-RELATED ACTIVITY.
- EXPELLED FROM SCHOOL AND SPENT TIME IN JUVENILE DETENTION.

GANG FOUNDING & CRIMES:

- IN 1971, CO-FOUNDED THE WEST SIDE CRIPS WITH RAYMOND WASHINGTON.
- ON FEBRUARY 28, 1979, PARTICIPATED IN THE ROBBERY AND MURDER OF A CONVENIENCE STORE CLERK.
- ON MARCH 11, 1979, WAS INVOLVED IN THE ROBBERY AND MURDER OF A MOTEL OWNER AND HIS FAMILY.
- CONVICTED OF FOUR COUNTS OF FIRST-DEGREE MURDER IN 1981 AND SENTENCED TO DEATH.

TRANSFORMATION & ADVOCACY:

- WHILE INCARCERATED, RENOUNCED GANG LIFE AND BECAME AN ANTI-GANG ACTIVIST.
- AUTHORED A SERIES OF CHILDREN'S BOOKS WARNING AGAINST GANG INVOLVEMENT.
- PUBLISHED A MEMOIR, BECAME A FIVE-TIME NOBEL PEACE PRIZE NOMINEE, AND RECEIVED NUMEROUS AWARDS FOR YOUTH OUTREACH.
- ADVOCATED FOR, AND HELPED TO BROKER GANG TRUCES, BECOMING A SYMBOL OF REHABILITATION.

EXECUTION:

- WIDESPREAD APPEALS FOR CLEMENCY CAME FROM RELIGIOUS LEADERS, ACTIVISTS, CELEBRITIES, AND EVEN FORMER GANG MEMBERS.
- CALIFORNIA GOVERNOR ARNOLD SCHWARZENEGGER DENIED CLEMENCY.
- EXECUTED BY LETHAL INJECTION ON DECEMBER 13, 2005, AT SAN QUENTIN.

CONVICTED OF 4 MURDERS IN 1981.

SPENT 24 YEARS ON DEATH ROW.

EXECUTED BY LETHAL INJECTION ON DECEMBER 13, 2005, AT SAN QUENTIN.

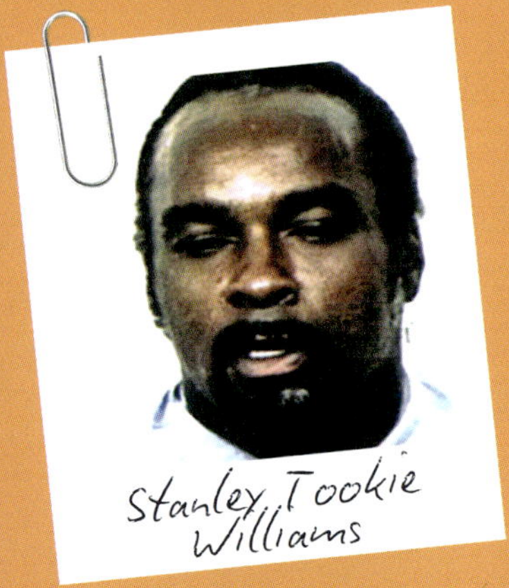

CRIME: MURDER
STATE: CALIFORNIA
YEAR: 2005
PUNISHMENT: LETHAL INJECTION

REQUESTED LAST MEAL:

DECLINED A SPECIAL MEAL, BUT HAD OATMEAL AND MILK BEFORE HIS EXECUTION.

OATMEAL AND MILK

INGREDIENTS:

- 240ML|1 CUP WATER
- PINCH KOSHER SALT
- 45G|1/2 CUP ROLLED OATS
- 240-355ML|1-1½ CUP WHOLE MILK
- SWEETENER OF CHOICE
- TOPPINGS, AS DESIRED

OATMEAL AND MILK

1. START WITH WATER

- BRING WATER TO A BOIL.
- ADD OATS AND A PINCH OF SALT.
- REDUCE HEAT AND SIMMER UNTIL WATER REDUCES AND OATS START TO SOFTEN

2. ADD MILK & SIMMER

- ADD MILK AND BRING TO A SIMMER (OR GENTLY BOIL).
- REDUCE HEAT AND COOK FOR ABOUT 10 MINUTES, STIRRING OCCASIONALLY TO PREVENT STICKING.

3. ADJUST & SERVE

- COOK UNTIL CREAMY BUT POURABLE.
- IF TOO THICK, ADD A SPLASH OF MILK TO LOOSEN.
- SERVE WARM WITH YOUR FAVORITE TOPPINGS.

BIOGRAPHY-ROBERT LEE MASSIE

ROBERT LEE MASSIE (1941-2001) WAS EXECUTED IN CALIFORNIA FOR A 1979 ROBBERY-MURDER, BUT HIS CASE STOOD OUT DUE TO ITS LONG, COMPLEX LEGAL HISTORY AND A PRIOR DEATH SENTENCE THAT HAD ONCE BEEN OVERTURNED. HE SPENT NEARLY FOUR DECADES ENTANGLED IN THE CRIMINAL JUSTICE SYSTEM, AND HIS EXECUTION MARKED ONE OF THE RARE INSTANCES OF A VOLUNTARY WAIVER OF APPEALS IN A MODERN CAPITAL CASE.

Robert Lee Massie

BORN:	4/12/1941
DIED:	03/27/2001 (AGED 59)
CONVICTIONS:	FIRST-DEGREE MURDER
PENALTY:	DEATH

EARLY LIFE:

- BORN DECEMBER 24, 1941, IN VIRGINIA.
- RAISED IN A TROUBLED AND ABUSIVE HOUSEHOLD; ENDURED SIGNIFICANT TRAUMA AND INSTABILITY DURING CHILDHOOD.
- SUFFERED FROM EMOTIONAL AND PSYCHOLOGICAL ISSUES, INCLUDING SIGNS OF ANTISOCIAL PERSONALITY DISORDER.

THE CRIMES:

- IN 1965, MASSIE COMMITTED A ROBBERY IN LOS ANGELES DURING WHICH HE SHOT TWO PEOPLE, KILLING ONE AND SERIOUSLY INJURING THE OTHER.
- CONVICTED OF FIRST-DEGREE MURDER AND SENTENCED TO DEATH IN 1965.
- THAT SENTENCE WAS OVERTURNED IN 1972 AFTER THE DEATH PENALTY WAS RULED UNCONSTITUTIONAL; HIS SENTENCE WAS COMMUTED TO LIFE.
- ON JANUARY 3, 1979, WHILE ON PAROLE, HE ATTEMPTED TO ROB A LIQUOR STORE IN SAN FRANCISCO AND FATALLY SHOT THE OWNER, BORIS G. NAUMOFF.
- ARRESTED AND CONFESSED TO THE CRIME.

ARREST & TRIAL:

- TRIED AND CONVICTED OF FIRST-DEGREE MURDER FOR THE KILLING OF NAUMOFF – HE WAS ONE OF THE FEW INDIVIDUALS IN U.S. HISTORY TO RECEIVE TWO SEPARATE DEATH SENTENCES FOR TWO DIFFERENT MURDERS.
- AT VARIOUS POINTS, HE ATTEMPTED TO WAIVE HIS APPEALS AND EXPEDITE HIS EXECUTION.

EXECUTION:

- AFTER YEARS OF LITIGATION, MASSIE ULTIMATELY DROPPED HIS REMAINING APPEALS.
- EXECUTED BY LETHAL INJECTION ON MARCH 27, 2001, AT SAN QUENTIN STATE PRISON.
- HE BECAME THE FOURTH PERSON EXECUTED IN CALIFORNIA AFTER THE STATE REINSTATED THE DEATH PENALTY IN 1978.
- AT THE TIME OF HIS EXECUTION, HE EXPRESSED REMORSE AND TOLD THE VICTIM'S FAMILY HE WAS SORRY.

CONVICTED OF MURDER IN 1979

SPENT 21 YEARS ON DEATH ROW

EXECUTED BY LETHAL INJECTION ON DECEMBER 13, 2005, AT SAN QUENTIN.

LAST MEAL–ROBERT LEE MASSIE

Robert Lee Massie

CRIME: MURDER
STATE: CALIFORNIA
YEAR: 2004
PUNISHMENT: LETHAL INJECTION

REQUESTED LAST MEAL:

TWO VANILLA MILKSHAKES, EXTRA CRISPY FRENCH FRIES, EXTRA CRISPY FRIED OYSTERS, AND SOFT DRINKS.

CRISPY FRIED OYSTERS

INGREDIENTS:

- 2 QUARTS VEGETABLE OIL, FOR FRYING
- 60G|1/2 CUP ALL-PURPOSE FLOUR
- 1 TEASPOON SALT
- 1/2 TEASPOON GROUND BLACK PEPPER
- 2 LARGE EGGS, LIGHTLY BEATEN
- 80G|3/4 CUP FINE BREADCRUMBS
- 340G|12 OZ SHUCKED OYSTERS, DRAINED

LAST MEAL

CRISPY FRIED OYSTERS

1. HEAT OIL

- HEAT OIL IN A DEEP FRYER TO 190°C |375°F.

2. SET UP BREADING STATIONS

- IN ONE BOWL, MIX FLOUR, SALT, AND PEPPER.
- IN A SECOND BOWL, BEAT THE EGGS.
- IN A THIRD BOWL, ADD BREAD CRUMBS.

3. BREAD THE OYSTERS

- DREDGE OYSTERS IN FLOUR MIXTURE, DIP IN EGG, THEN COAT WITH BREAD CRUMBS.

4. FRY THE OYSTERS

- FRY IN BATCHES OF 5 FOR ABOUT 2 MINUTES, UNTIL GOLDEN BROWN.
- DRAIN ON PAPER TOWELS.

5. SERVE HOT

- ENJOY WHILE CRISPY AND FRESH!

ROBERT MASSIE WAS CALIFORNIA'S LONGEST SERVING DEATH ROW INMATE AT TIME OF DEATH
-21 YEARS 10 MONTHS